Remarried
Family
Relationships

SAGE SERIES ON CLOSE RELATIONSHIPS

Series Editors
Clyde Hendrick, Ph.D., and
Susan S. Hendrick, Ph.D.

In this series...

Remarried Family Relationships

Lawrence H. Ganong
Marilyn Coleman

SS
CR
Sage
Series
on Close
Relationships

 SAGE Publications
International Educational and Professional Publisher
Thousand Oaks   London   New Delhi

For information address:

SAGE Publications, Inc.
2455 Teller Road
Thousand Oaks, California 91320

SAGE Publications Ltd.
6 Bonhill Street
London EC2A 4PU
United Kingdom

SAGE Publications India Pvt. Ltd.
M-32 Market
Greater Kailash I
New Delhi 110 048 India

Printed in the United States of America

Library of Congress Cataloging-in-Publication Data

Ganong, Lawrence H.
   Remarried family relationships / Lawrence H. Ganong, Marilyn Coleman.
      p.   cm.—(Sage series on close relationships)
   Includes bibliographical references and indexes.
   ISBN 0-8039-5122-1 (cl.).—ISBN 0-8039-5123-X (pbk.)
   1. Remarried people—United States—Family relationships.
   2. Stepfamilies—United States. 3. Remarriage—United States.
   I. Coleman, Marilyn. II. Title. III. Series.
   HQ1019.U6G36   1994
   306.84—dc20   94-1368

94 95 96 97 98   10 9 8 7 6 5 4 3 2 1

Sage Production Editor: Yvonne Könneker

Contents

Series Editors' Introduction

When we first began our work on love attitudes more than a decade ago, we did not know what to call our research area. In some ways it represented an extension of earlier work in interpersonal attraction. Most of our scholarly models were psychologists (though sociologists had long been deeply involved in the areas of courtship and marriage), yet we sometimes thought our work had no professional "home." That has all changed. Our research not only has a home, but it also has an extended family, and the family is composed of relationship researchers. During the past decade the discipline of close relationships (also called personal relationships and intimate relationships) has emerged, developed, and flourished.

Two aspects of close relationships research should be noted. The first is its rapid growth, resulting in numerous books, journals, handbooks, book series, and professional organizations. But as fast as the field grows, the demand for even more research and knowledge seems to be ever increasing. Questions about close, personal relationships still far exceed answers. The second noteworthy aspect of the new discipline of close relationships is its interdisciplinary nature. The field owes its vitality to scholars from communications, family studies and human development, psychology (clinical, counseling, developmental, social), and sociology, as well as other disciplines such as nursing and social work. It is this interdisciplinary wellspring that gives close relationships research its diversity and richness, qualities that we hope to achieve in this series.

The **Sage Series on Close Relationships** is designed to acquaint diverse readers with the most up-to-date information about various topics in close relationships theory and research. Each volume in the series covers a particular topic or theme in one area of close relationships. Each book reviews the particular topic area, describes contemporary research in the area (including the authors' own work, where appropriate), and offers some suggestions for interesting research questions and/or real-world applications related to the topic. The volumes are designed to be appropriate for students and professionals in communication, family studies, psychology, sociology, and social work, among others. A basic assumption of the series is that the broad panorama of close relationships can best be portrayed by authors from multiple disciplines, so that the series cannot be "captured" by any single disciplinary bias.

During the past decade Larry Ganong and Marilyn Coleman have become perhaps the most visible scholarly spokespersons for the remarried family, and this volume makes it clear why this renown has occurred. In this book, *Remarried Family Relationships*, Ganong and Coleman offer a timely and comprehensive look at remarried families, including perspectives on pathways from divorce to remarriage, key relationships in remarried families (including partners, stepparents and stepchildren, biological parents and children, and grandparents), and early and contemporary research on remarried couples and families. The volume is both scholarly and eminently readable as it addresses the myriad issues that confront today's many remarried families. It is the authors' perspective that remarried families offer a family form deserving of understanding, acceptance, and nurture. The editors wholeheartedly agree.

CLYDE HENDRICK
SUSAN S. HENDRICK
SERIES EDITORS

Preface

Although it may seem as if social scientists discovered the existence of remarried families relatively recently, this family form, also known as stepfamilies, has been common throughout history. Prior to the past 20 years or so, the death of a spouse was the most common precursor of remarriage, and the typical response of remarried parents was to attempt to recreate the nuclear family. This act was considered to be the normal thing to do at the time, and it was probably fairly successful when two adults were needed for families to survive. However, this strategy tends to work less well now that divorce is the most common precursor to remarriage. We have not been very creative in adapting to the added complexity created by stepchildren having more than two parenting figures in their lives, and, as a result, stepfamilies often are considered to be a problem in our society.

Social scientists have reinforced the problem-oriented perspective by using what we call a "deficit-comparison paradigm" in approaching the study of stepfamilies. In this paradigm stepfamilies and stepfamily members, particularly stepchildren, are compared with nuclear families and nuclear family members. The implicit assumption behind many (but certainly not all) of these deficit-comparison studies is that stepfamilies and stepchildren are somehow deficient, compared with adults and children in first-marriage families.

The deficit-comparison approach has been attributed, in part, to the fact that most of the early writing on stepfamilies was done by clinicians, those professionals most likely to see stepfamilies who were having problems. However, it was a pair of clinicians, John and Emily Visher, who were most influential in introducing a new paradigm in stepfamily research, the *normative-adaptive perspective*. The appearance of their book *Stepfamilies: A Guide to Working With Stepparents and Stepchildren* (1979) generated huge interest in stepfamilies among clinicians and researchers alike.

The normative-adaptive perspective does not deny the possibility of problems in stepfamilies, nor does it preclude comparing stepfamilies with other family forms. The main emphasis is not on problems or deficits, however, nor are comparisons with nuclear families the predominant research design. Rather, social scientists who take this paradigm will focus more on attempts to examine why some remarriages and some stepfamilies function well but others do not. The normative-adaptive perspective is the one taken in this book.

In Chapter 1 we present a brief history of the field of stepfamily study, provide current demographic information, describe a few stepfamily typologies, and present an overview of clinical, research, and theoretical approaches to stepfamily investigation. Chapter 2 contains a demographic overview of who remarries and a discussion of the three pathways to remarriage: divorce, bereavement, and never-married. Included in Chapter 3 are an overview of research and theory on remarried relationships, information about remarriage courtship process and behaviors, and a discussion of factors contributing to remarriage instability. Chapter 4 is concerned with the stepparent-stepchild relationship. Attention is paid to residential and nonresidential stepparent-stepchild relationships, and stepmother-stepchild and stepfather-stepchild relationships are discussed. The chapter closes with a review of the current information on child abuse in stepfamilies. Other stepfamily relationships are presented in Chapter 5, including several that are unique to remarried families. Relationships discussed include residential and nonresidential parent-child ties, siblings, half-siblings, and stepsiblings, grandparents, stepgrandparents, and those of the former spouses. Chapter 6 follows with a review of various clinical perspectives that provide insight into well-functioning and dysfunctional stepfamilies. Clinical models developed by Mills, McGoldrick and Carter, Papernow, and Visher and Visher are presented. Chapter 7, or the epilogue, closes the book by examining a relatively new model for conceptualizing close relationships in stepfamilies and providing insight into where the field is going. Identification of needed research is included as well.

This book would not have been possible without the support of several people during the past several years. In listing colleagues who have helped influence our thinking about stepfamilies, we realize we run the risk of overlooking some. However, we are especially grateful to John and Emily Visher, Kay Pasley, Marilyn Ihinger-Tallman, Larry Kurdek, Mark Fine, Glenn Clingempeel, Margaret Crosbie-Burnett, Patricia Papernow, Connie Ahrons, and Jean Giles-Sims for their continued friendship and collegiality. We are also appreciative of the support given to us by the editors of this **Sage Series on Close Relationships**, Clyde and Susan Hendrick. We cannot imagine more cooperative editors. Finally we want to thank the stepfamily members who have participated in our research during the last few years. In particular we are deeply indebted to the 105 mid-Missouri stepfamilies who, in 1984 and again in 1988, shared intimate details of their lives with us and greatly enriched our understanding of stepfamily dynamics.

1

The Context
of Remarried Families

In the 1950s Betty Friedan revived the feminist movement by writing of "the problem with no name." We are writing about "the families with no name"—or, to be more accurate, the families with no widely agreed on name.

The title of this book indicates that the focus is on remarried families. This label is but one of many that has been applied to the type of families we discuss. A review of professional literature would yield the following labels: reconstituted, blended, reconstructed, reorganized, reformed, recycled, combined, rem, step, second-time around, merged, and remarried families. None of these are totally satisfactory to us. Some seem awkward or even silly (e.g., *reconstituted* reminds people of orange juice, *blended* conjures images of whiskey), some are used inconsistently in the literature to describe different types of families (e.g., *blended* some-times is used specifically to refer to families in which both adults are stepparents, and sometimes it is used broadly to identify all remarried families), some are inaccurate as broad labels (e.g., not all are second-time around families, some are third- or fourth-time around, and a remarriage for one partner may be a first marriage for the other), some are too vague (e.g., *combined*), some carry negative connotations (e.g., *stepfamily*), and some suggest odd labels for individual family positions (e.g., a *reformed* or *reconsti-tuted* father, a *merged* or *reorganized* mother). Because none of these labels have won widespread approval by social and behavioral scientists, the selection of terms remains somewhat a personal choice. We use *remarried family* and *stepfamily* interchangeably.

Several labels have been applied to stepparents as well: nonpar-ents, half-parents, acquired parents, added parents, and second or third parents have been used in the professional literature (Espi-noza & Newman, 1979). We have heard stepparents call them-selves sociological parents, and many stepfamily members refer to stepparents simply as parents. Individual family positions in this book are identified as *biological parent or parent, stepparent,* and *child or stepchild.*

Just as "the problem with no name" was relatively unnoticed prior to Friedan's groundbreaking book, the families with too many names were relatively unnoticed until the 1980s, when the sheer force of numbers made it impossible to continue to ignore stepfamilies. There have always been remarried families; rates of remarriage in western Europe and the United States in the 18th century were similar to current remarriage rates (Chandler, 1991; Noy, 1991).

The sports chant popular in the United States, "We're number one," could also apply to marriage. We nearly all marry, and we marry often. In fact, the United States has the highest remarriage rate in the world: 40% of all marriages are remarriages for one or both partners (Chamie & Nsuly, 1981). We not only remarry at a high rate, we remarry quickly. The median interval between divorce and re-marriage is 3 years (Glick, 1980). Because two-thirds of all couples cohabit before remarriage (Bumpass & Sweet, 1989), the median interval from one relationship to another is indeed short.

Obviously all remarriages do not involve children. Census Bureau data are not available regarding the number of stepfamilies, and estimates vary widely. However, even the most conservative estimates indicate that stepfamilies make up a sizable minority of the population. Cherlin and McCarthy (1985) calculated that there are nearly 2.5 million postdivorce stepfamily households with residential children. To this number must be added an unknown number of remarriages formed after the death of a spouse, and de facto stepfamilies in which adults do not legally remarry (and consequently do not get counted by demographers). In addition, many single-parent households are linked to stepparent households; that is, most commonly, children live with their mother in a single-parent household and visit their father who is remarried.

According to demographer Paul Glick (1989), 19% of married couple families with children are stepfamilies, and one-third of Americans are now a stepparent, a stepchild, a stepsibling, or some other member of a stepfamily. At any one time about 10% of American children live with a stepfather and mother (Bumpass, 1984; Glick, 1984) and about 2% with a stepmother and father (Bachrach, 1983). If current rates of divorce and remarriage continue, as many as 35% of the children in the United States will be part of a stepfamily before they are 18 years old (Glick, 1989).

It is popular in modern American society to think of nuclear families as traditional families and to think of all others as nontraditional, or alternative, families (Coontz, 1992; Skolnick, 1991). These inaccurate labels convey the impression that families formed after remarriage are alternative family structures that have arisen relatively recently as a result of the increased divorce rate. Although it is true that divorce, rather than the death of a spouse, is now the most common precursor to remarriage, it is not true that remarried families are a recent phenomenon. Families formed as a result of marriages between adults who have children from previous relationships have existed in large numbers and in most cultures throughout history (see Spanier & Furstenberg, 1987, or Ihinger-Tallman & Pasley, 1987a or 1987b, for concise and informative historical reviews of remarried families). For example, George Washington, the father of our country, was also a stepfather. Abraham Lincoln was a stepchild, and it was his stepmother,

Nancy, who fostered his early interest in reading and learning. Most recently, presidents who were members of stepfamilies include Ford, Reagan, and Clinton.

Despite the large numbers of stepfamily members in our country, remarried families have not been extensively studied, and many unanswered questions remain. Much more needs to be known about close relationships within these families.

❧ Studying Close Relationships in Remarried Families

Close relationships within remarried families are among the most fascinating and most frustrating to study. The complexity of stepfamily relationships presents challenges to the researcher, scholar, and student. A simple example will illustrate what we mean. One problem that has plagued research and writing about remarriage and steprelationships has been confusion over what is, and is not, being studied. Defining who is being included in a study of remarried families is a more difficult task than one might think, and it certainly is more complicated than defining a sample of nuclear families.

Unlike nuclear families, remarried family members do not necessarily reside full-time in one household. In fact, with joint legal and physical custody of children after divorce becoming more prevalent in the United States, children's membership in two households is an increasingly common occurrence. Thus a remarried household may be linked with another remarried household or with a single-parent household by children (Jacobson, 1987), and these "binuclear" households may contain several combinations of full- and part-time steprelationships (Ahrons & Perlmutter, 1982). That households and families are not the same is only part of the complexity of defining remarried families, however. Roles and relationships within and across these families and households are incredibly complex, difficult to define, and ever changing.

Bohannon (1984) mentioned eight roles and eight possible dyadic relationships in the nuclear family identified by kinship terms recognized in English; husband-wife, father-son, father-daughter, mother-son, mother-daughter, brother-brother, sister-sister, and brother-sister. Death or divorce changes the family and household structure, resulting in vacant roles and absent dyadic relationships. When the divorced couple each remarry new spouses who already have children, a total of 22 dyadic relationships is possible. The stepfamily contains the typical family relationships (e.g., mother-son), but it also contains relationships never found in nuclear families (e.g., half-sister–half-brother). An additional difference mentioned by Bohannon (1984) is that stepfamily households are different from nuclear family households because they contain what anthropologists call affinal kin. *Affinal kin* are individuals related through the marriage of a family member. An example of a commonly known affinal kin is the mother-in-law. In the Western world mothers-in-law are negatively stereotyped and subject to ridicule. Stepchildren and stepparents are also affinal kin. They are in-laws in much the same way as mothers-in-law, except they are in the younger generation rather than the older generation.

Remarried Family Typologies

Remarried family structures are of several types. In efforts to help make the structural complexity more manageable for scholars, a number of researchers have identified typologies for conceptualizing the structural variations of remarried family life. Some of these structural typologies are shown in Table 1.1. For example, Clingempeel and colleagues developed a structural taxonomy based on two variables—the presence or absence of children from prior relationships, and the custody (residence) of those children—resulting in nine types of remarried families (Clingempeel, Brand, & Segal, 1987). Pasley and Ihinger-Tallman (1982) also postulated a nine-category typology based on presence or absence of children from either prior relationships or the present union, age of the children (adult or minor children), and custody (residence) of children from prior relationships. Wald (1981) identified 15 types of remarried family configurations based on the residence of children from the prior unions of both adults. The number of categories in Wald's typology doubles when children are born to the remarried couple.

Table 1.1 Three Structural Typologies for Remarried Families

Pasley & Ihinger-Tallman (1982)	Clingempeel, Brand, & Segal (1987)	Wald (1981) Children of Prior Unions	
		Husband	Wife
1. No children[a]	1. Remarried family[a] (if one or both spouses were married before)	1. All[b]	None[c]
2. Children of this marriage only[a]		2. All	Some/some elsewhere[d]
3. Custodial children from prior marriage only	2. Nonresidential stepmother family	3. All	All elsewhere[e]
		4. All	All
4. Noncustodial children from prior marriage only	3. Residential stepmother family	5. None	All
	4. Nonresidential stepfather family	6. Some/some elsewhere	All
5. Adult children only		7. All elsewhere	All
	5. Residential stepfather family	8. Some/some elsewhere	Some/some elsewhere
6. Custodial children from prior marriage and children from this marriage	6. Nonresidential stepparent family[f]	9. Some/some elsewhere	None
		10. All elsewhere	Some/some elsewhere
7. Noncustodial children from prior marriage and children from this marriage	7. Residential stepparent family[g]	11. None	Some/some elsewhere
	8. Mixed stepparent family (stepmother type)[h]	12. Some/some elsewhere	All elsewhere
8. Noncustodial and custodial children from prior marriage	9. Mixed stepparent family (stepfather type)[h]	13. All elsewhere	None
		14. None	All elsewhere
9. Noncustodial and custodial children from prior marriage and children from this marriage		15. All elsewhere	All elsewhere

a. A family type not covered in the definition of remarried families in this book.
b. All = Marital partner has children of a prior marriage, all of whom live in the remarried family household.
c. None = Marital partner has no children from prior marriage(s).
d. Some/some elsewhere = Marital partner has children of a prior marriage, some of whom live in the remarried family household and others who live elsewhere.
e. All elsewhere = Marital partner has children of a prior marriage, none of whom live in the remarried family household.
f. Both adults are parents to children of prior unions; all children live outside of the stepfamily household.
g. Both adults are parents to children of prior unions; all children live in stepfamily household.
h. Both adults are parents; only one set of children lives in household.

Before we leave this simple example of why studying stepfamilies is so challenging, we should point out that just as there is no single structural definition of stepfamilies, there is also no uniform psychological definition of stepfamily membership. For example, Gross (1987) asked stepchildren to identify who was in their family. Their responses fell into four categories that she labeled "retention," "substitution," "reduction," and "augmentation." In the *retention* group were children who psychologically retained both biological parents as family members and who were emotionally close to both their nonresidential and residential parent but not to a stepparent with whom they lived. The children in the *substitution* group replaced their nonresidential parent with the stepparent they lived with, so that household members only, regardless of biological ties, were considered to be family. In the *reduction* group, children included only one parent as part of their family, the one with whom they resided. The other parent and any stepparents were excluded. The final group, *augmentation,* contained those children who identified both parents and at least one stepparent as family. Gross (1987) cautioned researchers and clinicians to take into account children's perspectives on remarried family membership rather than to impose definitions on them; she argued that adherence to a view of remarried families as recreated nuclear families impedes professionals' understanding of these families.

Support for the idea of taking an eclectic, flexible definition of remarried families goes beyond the boundaries of the United States. For example, Australian stepchildren used a variety of criteria to decide who was in their family (Funder, 1991). Among the criteria were biological ties, sharing a household with the child, sharing a household with the child's nonresidential parent, and being important to the child for some reason. As Gross (1987) suggested, children in remarried families clearly construct definitions of family membership.

Adults cognitively construct their families as well; an amusing, albeit idiosyncratic, construction of family status was conveyed by Mary Catherine Bateson (1989), who stated in her book *Composing a Life* that her mother, the famous anthropologist Margaret Mead, only counted her previous marriages if the union produced either a child or a book! Most psychological definitions of family membership are less unique than Mead's.

Burgoyne and Clark (1984) developed a five-category typology based on how remarried adults thought of their families. Those in what they called "progressive stepfamilies" thought of themselves as stepfamilies and recognized that family membership extended beyond the household. Those in the category "looking forward to the departure of the children" accepted their stepfamily status as something different from that of nuclear families but longed for the point in the future when children were gone and interactions with former spouses were reduced. Stepfamilies who wanted to identify themselves and function as nuclear families were labeled "conscious pursuit of a nuclear family life frustrated" because former spouses and nonresidential children from prior relationships would not allow them to pretend to be nuclear families. Both of the final two groups in Burgoyne and Clark's typology thought of themselves as nuclear families and, as far as possible, functioned as nuclear families. In the "not really a stepfamily" group, stepchildren were young when the parent remarried, and often children were born of the remarriage union. In the largely successful "conscious pursuit of a nuclear family" group, stepparents had tried consciously and purposively to assume the role of parent, even going so far as transferring their allegiance from their nonresidential biological children to the stepchildren with whom they lived. Although we focus on the definitional aspects of this typology, it should be kept in mind that these cognitive constructions of their family status have enormous pragmatic importance in the day-to-day functioning of these families.

It is little wonder that the development of literature on close relationships in stepfamilies lags behind research in other areas, considering the complexity involved in even defining the population of interest. Before we proceed, it is important to define and explain what types of close relationships we are including under the rubric of "remarried families."

Defining Remarried Families

A *remarried family* is one in which at least one of the adults has a child or children from a previous relationship. A *stepparent* is an adult whose partner has at least one child from a previous relationship. A *stepchild* is a person whose parent or parents are partnered with someone who is not the child's biological or adoptive parent. Notice that these definitions do not limit remarried family status only to those who reside in the same household. A stepparent and stepchild do not have to live together all of the time, or even part of the time, to have a relationship together and to share remarried family membership.

The definitions above are not limited to legal marriages. Most research has focused on legal remarriages, probably because the date on which a couple files their marriage license is an easily measured marker of when the remarried family began. Limiting research to legal remarriages is unnecessary, however, for two reasons. First, many adults who live together and raise children, both from prior relationships and from their own union, do not legally marry. Statistics on these families are difficult to obtain, but evidence shows that such families are on the rise in the United States and elsewhere (Bumpass & Sweet, 1989). Second, most couples who legally remarry live together prior to remarriage (Bumpass & Sweet, 1989). We argue that living together is a better psychological and social marker of the beginning of a remarried family than is a definition based on legal remarriage. Researchers who measure the length of family life beginning with remarriage may miscalculate by months and even years for a majority of remarried families.

We want also to point out that the definitions we use are not limited to heterosexual unions. Homosexual couples in which one or both partners have children match our definition. Such families likely would have different dynamics from families headed by heterosexual couples, but there is also reason to think that many of the issues and dynamics would be similar (e.g., in steprelationships and former spouse relationships).

The definitions used in this book are broad because it is our intention to cover as much of the field as possible and to show areas in which more research and scholarly thought are needed. It will be obvious to the careful reader of this book, however, that most researchers and clinicians have assumed narrower definitions, and, in fact, the task of defining who is and is not in a remarried family can sometimes be controversial.

The controversy is related to the reason why there are so many definitions in the first place: value differences regarding families. Some scholars have difficulty conceptualizing family as any group other than one comprised of a mother, a father, and their biological children (i.e., the nuclear family). Because the nuclear family is the standard to which others are compared, the family form considered to be best for children and adults, other families are thought of and defined in contrast to nuclear families. Although, at some level, people realize that nuclear families are not all alike, the actual structure (i.e., mother, father, and children living in the same household) is basically the same, and it is simple. Because we think simplistically about nuclear family structure, the tendency is also to think simplistically about other families. This simplistic thinking, in the case of stepfamilies, has contributed to researchers and clinicians equating families and households (i.e., assuming they are the same entity) and has led to the exclusion of many families that we think should be included as stepfamilies. The equating of families and households also has contributed to researchers overlooking important close relationships such as those between nonresidential stepparents and stepchildren (e.g., those relationships between children who visit their biological father and their father's new wife, the children's stepmother, on holidays and alternating weekends).

❧ A Brief History of the Study of Remarried Families

In the remainder of this chapter, we present a brief history of the scholarly study of remarried families, a relatively easy task because most of the work has been done in the last 15 years. We also provide an overview of the theories and conceptual frameworks used to investigate close relationships in remarried families. This task is relatively easy as well because few attempts have been made to theorize about close relationships in remarried families until recently.

Examining the historical development of a field of scholarly inquiry can be instructive. For example, such an examination allows one to assess the relation between sociocultural and his-torical changes and changes in how social scientists think about and conduct research on a specific subject area (in this case, remarried families). Although researchers often are portrayed as impractical scientists working in an "ivory tower" independent of the cultural and historical forces that influence the rest of society, for social scientists who study close relationships, this is a myth. In practice, social and behavioral researchers generally are firmly entrenched in their cultural time and place and are reinforced by a variety of influences, such as funding agencies that are respond-ing to social trends and concerns; colleagues who review manu-scripts for journals, editors, tenure committees; and what has been called the "invisible college" (Crane, 1972), the community of scholars who study and write about the same topic.

૭ The Study of Remarried Families Prior to 1980

Research and Theory

Although remarried families have existed in many cultures for centuries, the study of close relationships in remarried families is a surprisingly recent phenomenon. Prior to the late 1970s, researchers showed little interest in remarried families. The first study in North America on remarriage was published in the 1930s (Waller, 1930), a few studies appeared in the decade following World War II (e.g., Bernard, 1956; Landis, 1950; Smith, 1953), and a handful were pub-lished in the 1960s and 1970s (e.g., Bowerman & Irish, 1962; Duber-man, 1975). As recently as 1979, a review of the literature yielded only 11 empirical studies on stepfamilies, including unpublished doctoral dissertations. These studies had sampled a total of only 550 step-families in the United States (Espinoza & Newman, 1979).

Obviously such a small body of research was limited in the dimensions of remarried family life that were investigated. For the most part the early studies focused either on the well-being of stepchildren or on stepparent-stepchild relationships. After re-viewing the extant literature, Furstenberg (1979) identified 10 topics needing further study:

1. Consequences of prior marital experience on the remarriage transition
2. Effects of divorce adjustment on remarriage
3. Effects of remarriage on other life course events and experiences
4. Effects of remarriage on self-image and self-identity
5. Changes in conjugal relations following remarriage
6. Remarriage effects on perceptions of social reality
7. Relationships between former spouses after the remarriage of one or both former partners
8. How child-rearing functions are fulfilled
9. How ties with old extended kin are maintained
10. How ties are initiated with new extended kin

Each item on this list represents literally dozens of potential research questions.

The early research was limited conceptually and methodologically. There were no longitudinal investigations, few that had large, representative samples of remarried families, and few in which standardized measures were used (Price-Bonham & Balswick, 1980). The majority of studies were atheoretical and descriptive.

One major exception to the atheoretical work in the 1970s was Andrew Cherlin's (1978) article "Remarriage as an Incomplete Institution." Cherlin argued that remarried families after divorce have more difficulties than first-marriage families because they lack institutionalized guidelines and support to help them solve their family problems. He further concluded that the absence of guidelines and norms for role performance; the dearth of culturally established, socially acceptable methods of resolving problems; and the relative absence of institutionalized social support for remarried adults and stepparents contribute to greater stress, inappropriate solutions to problems, and higher divorce rates for remarried families. Cherlin pointed to language and legal regulations as illustrations of how remarriages are incompletely institutionalized. Earlier in this chapter we mentioned some of the problems with identifying culturally agreed on labels for remarried families and positions within remarried families; Cherlin argued that this confusion of labels was a consequence of the incomplete institutionalization of remarried families.

Cherlin's frequently cited, heavily influential article stimulated several studies of remarried families since its publication (cf.

Booth & Edwards, 1992; Clingempeel, 1981; Giles-Sims, 1984; Hobart, 1989). The assertions Cherlin made were provocative and lend themselves to empirical testing by a variety of methods and designs. Several of the studies based on the incomplete institutionalization hypothesis are discussed in later chapters, so for now we only say that considerable support has been found for Cherlin's (1978) argument.

Clinical Perspectives

While the social scientific community slowly developed a body of research on the dynamics of remarried families, the applied community of clinicians, including clinical psychologists, social workers, and psychiatrists, were more rapidly building a corpus of literature on the problems confronting remarried couples, stepparents, and stepchildren. In fact, it would be fair to say that the writing and thinking of clinicians dominated the early (pre-1980) literature. One consequence of this early domination of the stepfamily literature by clinicians may have been the reinforcement of beliefs that such families are inherently problematic. Clinicians, basing their views on individuals, couples, and families encountering intrapersonal and interpersonal difficulties, naturally focused on the pathological elements of remarried family life. This emphasis on family problems and pathology may have helped set the tone for later research efforts, although evidence shows that researchers do not generally consult clinical literature (Ganong & Coleman, 1986).

Several clinicians, such as Lillian Messinger and her colleagues (Messinger, 1976; Messinger, Walker, & Freeman, 1978), were influential in shaping this literature, but late in the decade it was the work of Emily and John Visher (1979) that most influenced how the dynamics of stepfamily life were conceptualized. The Vishers, clinicians who were stepparents themselves, began writing extensively and lecturing nationwide to stepfamily members and clinicians during the 1970s. They also founded the Stepfamily Association of America, a national self-help and support group for stepfamily members. The Vishers' clearly articulated perspectives on remarriage and stepfamily functioning have had broad appeal to stepfamily members, clinicians, and researchers. Their asserted beliefs that stepfamilies functioned differently from first-marriage families and should be conceptualized as having unique relationships and patterns of interactions have been influential. They were also among the first to focus on strengths of stepfamily living, as well as problems, serving as a counterbalance to the generally pervasive, problem-oriented views.

❧ The Study of Remarried Families in the 1980s

Research and Theory

The decade of the 1980s witnessed an explosion of scholarly interest in remarriage, stepparenting, and stepfamilies. Coleman and Ganong (1990) located "well over 200" published studies from the 1980s for a decade review; Pasley and Ihinger-Tallman (1992) reviewed 284 studies conducted in the 1980s; and Ihinger-Tallman (1988) found 95 dissertations written on remarriage and stepparenting between 1980 and 1987. Theoretical works also increased, as did publications with applied foci.

The decade not only was the most productive period for research on remarriage and stepfamilies, but during this era the quality of the investigations improved as well. The 1980s could be thought of as two distinct periods, 1980-1984 and 1985-1989. The body of scholarly work on remarried families done in the second half of the decade differed in several ways from that of the first half.

1980-1984. Remarried families attracted more attention from researchers in the first half of the 1980s than in the previous 50 years combined. However, the research continued to be plagued with inconsistencies and methodological problems, including:

- little use of theory
- limited assessment of stepfamily structural variables
- failure to account for the complexity of stepfamilies
- small and nonrandom samples
- overreliance on self-report questionnaires of unknown validity and reliability

- use of data gathered from only one family member (Esses & Campbell, 1984; Ganong & Coleman, 1984)

Moreover, this body of literature was criticized because a "deficit-comparison" approach was most commonly taken to the study of remarried families, an atheoretical assumption that steprelationships would function at a deficit, compared with relationships in nuclear families (Ganong & Coleman, 1984). This assumption led to (a) using nuclear families as comparison groups even when it was not appropriate to do so, (b) interpreting differences as deficits, and (c) applying inappropriate norms to relationships in remarried families. The deficit-comparison perspective is not unique to research on remarried families; one can find similar trends in research on single-parent families, African American families, and dual career couples, suggesting perhaps that using the nuclear family as the standard for comparison is part of the development of an area of inquiry. It remains to be seen whether the deficit perspective is reduced in importance when more sophisticated thinking and theorizing are available.

In separate reviews of the research conducted prior to 1984, several critical needs for stepfamily research were identified:

1. Longitudinal studies, preferably beginning prior to remarriage
2. Efforts to control for or measure crucial variables such as custody arrangements and length of remarriage
3. Larger samples or limits to the structural types of stepfamilies included in each study, so that differences in types of stepfamilies could be compared
4. Use of multiple methods of data collection
5. Greater use of theory
6. Research on the development of relationships in stepfamilies
7. Studies of stepfamilies with children of different ages
8. More research on stepmother families
9. Descriptive studies of well-functioning stepfamilies (Esses & Campbell, 1984; Ganong & Coleman, 1984)

This extensive list echoed the earlier critical reviews (Furstenberg, 1979; Price-Bonham & Balswick, 1980), but a careful reading of the 1984 suggestions reveals that remarried family scholars were becoming more sophisticated in their thinking and perhaps even more demanding of their colleagues. At least some researchers clearly were anxious to abandon the well-trod ground of the oversimplified deficit-comparison designs in favor of exploring new territory with new maps.

In the early years of this decade, some of the areas of research on close relationships in remarried families were characterized by "whoozle effects," in which generalizations were drawn from very little evidence (Ganong & Coleman, 1986). According to Gelles (1980), a whoozle effect occurs when a particular finding reported in one study is cited subsequently by others without consideration of possible limitations to the study and without efforts to replicate the findings. Frequent citations of a study result in the findings being treated as more solidly confirmed by data than is actually the case, and original caveats regarding study limitations are forgotten. Whoozle effects are more likely when a body of literature is not comprehensive and when there are few studies to cite. Such was the case of research on remarried family relationships in the early 1980s.

1985-1989. The concerns about stepfamily research that were identified in 1984 had begun to be addressed by researchers in the last half of the decade (Coleman & Ganong, 1990; Pasley & Ihinger-Tallman, 1992). A few longitudinal studies had been launched, more researchers were trying to account for the complexity of stepfamily structures, large national samples had been examined, some researchers were using multilevel-multivariable-multimeasure designs, indications were that greater attention was being paid to theory, and, compared with the beginning of the decade, there was more information about previously understudied topics such as stepmother-stepchild relationships.

The Rise of Theory. Much of the research continued to be either atheoretical or based on the deficit-comparison assumption. In the later years of the decade, however, more attempts were made to test theoretical propositions, and some beginning efforts were made to build theory related to remarriage and stepfamilies. The range of theories represented in this work was broad, reflecting the diverse, multidisciplinary nature of the scholars who focused their energies on understanding close relationships in remarried families. Among the major theories were social exchange (Giles-Sims, 1987b; Giles-Sims & Crosbie-Burnett, 1989; Zick & Smith, 1988), family systems (Coleman & Ganong, 1987b; Crosbie-Burnett, 1984), sociobiology (Flinn, 1988; Lightcap, Kurland, & Burgess, 1982), social learning (Coleman & Ganong, 1984; Ganong, Coleman, & Brown, 1981; Kiecolt & Acock, 1988), role (Fox & Inazu, 1982; Giles-Sims, 1984), and feminist theory (Crosbie-Burnett, Skyles, & Becker-Haven, 1988). More recently, social cognitive theories have been applied to stepfamily relationships (Fine, Donnelly, & Voydanoff, 1991; Fine & Schwebel, 1991; Kurdek, 1991a; Kurdek & Fine, 1993).

Several middle-range theories also were tested. *Middle-range theories* commonly are defined as "modest in scope and generality, relatively close to data, easily tested and easily revised" (Holman & Burr, 1980, p. 733). Olson's circumplex model (Pink & Wampler, 1985), Becker's economic model of marriage (Michael & Tuma, 1985; Mott & Moore, 1983), Baumrind's model of parenting styles (Dornbusch, Ritter, Leiderman, Roberts, & Fraleigh, 1987), and McCubbin's double ABCX model of family stress (Crosbie-Burnett, 1989a) were among the middle-range theories that guided stepfamily research. Several models of stepfamily development also were proposed (Hill, 1986; Mills, 1984; Papernow, 1984; Whiteside, 1982) but were not tested empirically. In addition to the "incomplete institution hypothesis" (Cherlin, 1978), several other hypotheses were tested, including the socialization hypothesis (Booth, Brinkerhoff, & White, 1984; Kinnaird & Gerrard, 1986; McLanahan & Bumpass, 1988), the economic deprivation hypothesis (Michael & Tuma, 1985), and the stress hypothesis (McLanahan & Bumpass, 1988).

The latter half of the decade saw several attempts to generate theory specific to remarried families. Both inductive theories (Gross, 1987; Roberts & Price, 1987) and deductive, propositional theories were developed (Ihinger-Tallman, 1987; Rodgers & Conrad, 1986). These efforts make it likely that theory testing will be one of the main thrusts of remarriage and stepfamily research in the 1990s.

Clinical Perspectives

Bold strides were also made in clinical scholarship during the 1980s. In fact, practitioners continued to publish more voluminously than did researchers and theorists (Ganong & Coleman, 1986). New strategies for working with remarried families were developed, while established techniques were elaborated (cf. Sager et al., 1983; Visher & Visher, 1988). Advances occurred in how remarried families were conceptualized as well (cf. Mills, 1984; Papernow, 1984, 1987).

Unfortunately, clinicians and researchers tended not to consult each other's work. In a comparison of the clinical and empirical literature on stepchildren, Ganong and Coleman (1986) found little congruence between the two literatures, concluding, "There is much evidence to indicate that researchers and clinicians interested in stepchildren are professionally segregated and little evidence demonstrating communication between the groups" (p. 315). We thought then that both clinical practice and research would be enhanced if there was greater communication between the two groups of professionals, a perspective that we continue to hold (see Chapter 6).

The Development of an Area of Study

Several events occurred during the decade of the 1980s that were both consequences of the growing interest in remarried families and helpful in spurring further development of research in this area of study. In 1982 an interdisciplinary group of scholars formed a Focus Group on Remarriage and Stepparenting within the National Council on Family Relations. Initially organized to facilitate networking and information exchange, this group initiated and has maintained a comprehensive bibliography of research, theory, and applied publications on remarriage and stepparenting. The group continues to meet annually.

In 1983 the Society for Research in Child Development funded an interdisciplinary study group of scholars interested in the effects of remarriage on children, a project that resulted in an edited book of theory and research (Pasley & Ihinger-Tallman,

1987). In 1987 another interdisciplinary group was convened, the Wingspread Conference on Remarried Families, sponsored by the Stepfamily Association of America (SAA), the American Family Therapy Association (AFTA), the National Council on Family Relations (NCFR), and the American Association of Marriage and Family Therapy (AAMFT). The Wingspread Conference was to be a one-time meeting but has evolved into an informal network of researchers, clinicians, and policymakers who meet annually at either NCFR or AAMFT conferences. One notable outcome of the Wingspread group was to convince the editor and publisher of the *Journal of Divorce* to rename it the *Journal of Divorce and Remarriage*, a name change that took place in 1990.

The growing recognition of remarried family life as an area worthy of more focus by researchers was seen not only in the increased number of publications in the 1980s but also in the special issues of journals devoted to remarriage and stepparenting (*Journal of Family Issues*, 1980, 1992; *Family Relations*, 1984, 1989). It is fair to suggest that in the 1980s remarried families emerged as a clearly identified area of investigation, partly because researchers and clinicians made a strong case for the uniqueness of the dynamics in such families.

Although only a few of the questions raised by Furstenberg in 1979 had been answered by 1990, the 1980s clearly were a time of exciting methodological, conceptual, and empirical progress in the study of remarried families. Pasley and Ihinger-Tallman (1992) concluded, after comparing the research literature to the recommendations made in earlier critical reviews (Esses & Campbell, 1984; Furstenberg, 1979; Ganong & Coleman, 1984), that researchers had "given serious attention to the many recommendations" but still "have a long way to go in effectively addressing the theoretical and methodological limitations noted" (p. 166).

We discuss the limitations of the research on close relationships in remarried families at length later in this volume. For now, we simply note the main problems characterizing this body of work at the end of the 1980s. First, the deficit-comparison approach was still prevalent. As a result of the adherence to this nuclear family ideology, inadequate attention was given to the structural complexity and diversity of stepfamilies, attention was focused mainly on problems in relationships rather than on positive interactions, and stephouseholds and stepfamilies were conceptualized as equivalent units. Researchers also generally ignored the influences of events that occurred prior to remarriage, influences we think are so important that we discuss them at length in Chapter 2. The reactivity of measures and methods, and the difficulty in obtaining representative samples of remarried families were also problems characteristic of the research in this decade (Coleman & Ganong, 1990). In the Epilogue of this volume we suggest directions that the field should take in the 1990s and beyond.

≈ Overall Development of a Field of Study

Why were researchers so slow in addressing close relationships in remarried families? One possibility is that social scientists were unaware of the large numbers of stepfamilies, although more than 40 years ago Paul Landis (1950) described the state of American families as one of "sequential polygamy." Landis noted that multiple marriages were more common in our culture than in some cultures described as polygamous. In the late 1960s or early 1970s, anthropologist Margaret Mead wrote of "serial monogamy" (one partner follows another) as the coming norm in American families (Mead, 1970). So it seems that at least some social scientists were aware of the increasing number of remarried families. Lack of awareness is probably not a sufficient explanation for the dearth of research on stepfamily relationships.

Furstenberg (1979) speculated that remarried families were neglected as an area of study because midlife remarriage violates culturally expected "normative schedules" of movement into and out of social positions over the life course. Furstenberg argued that family scholars generally have been reluctant to see divorce and remarriage as normative changes in the kinship system rather than as aberrations to accepted cultural practices. Similarly, Gerald Leslie (1976) attributed the paucity of research prior to the mid-1970s as a consequence of adherence to a family ideology that marriages should be permanent until one of the partners died. Both Furstenberg and Leslie were suggesting that values held by researchers contributed to the relatively slow development of step-family research. They contended that stepfamilies were ignored by researchers because they were seen as violating accepted cultural practices. These cultural practices were presumably also part of the belief systems of most researchers. This argument is less than compelling, however, because researchers were actively studying divorce at the same time they were ignoring remarried families.

This is not to suggest that scientists' values are not relevant or influential. However, researchers' values probably have affected the direction or content of stepfamily research more than the quality of research or the pace at which the body of research developed; that is, researchers' values, opinions, and beliefs likely influenced the types of issues addressed, the way hypotheses and research questions were worded, the selection of samples and measurement instruments, and interpretations of the meaning of data (see Miller, 1993, and Thompson, 1992, for excellent discussions of the roles that values play in family research in general). Despite attempts by social science researchers to limit biases in their research designs, the fact that they have values and beliefs about families may introduce subtle biases into their investigations. It would be naive to assume that social science researchers are not influenced by cultural ideologies and belief systems about family life (Clingempeel, Flescher, & Brand, 1987; Coleman & Ganong, 1987a; Collins, 1991).

Epistemic and Nonepistemic Values in Stepfamily Research

Clingempeel, Flescher, and Brand (1987), in a review of the research on stepfamilies from a constructivist perspective, identified what they termed "paradigmatic constraints" on the development of this body of knowledge. The *constructivist perspective* holds that all knowledge is invented, rather than discovered, and is based on the beliefs and cognitions of researchers, rather than on a single set of objective facts (Gergen, 1985). The belief systems of researchers are based partly on the values and beliefs they have been taught as scientists regarding how research should be conducted (epistemic beliefs and values) and partly on personal values and beliefs (nonepistemic beliefs). Applied to family research, Clingempeel and his colleagues defined *nonepistemic values* as attitudes about what is good or bad for families, and *epistemic values* as the best methods for conducting research on families. Both epistemic and nonepistemic values of social scientists are influenced by sociocultural and historical factors.

We already have mentioned some nonepistemic constraints on stepfamily research: the belief that nuclear families are the standard by which all other family forms should be compared, and the belief that remarried families are cultural aberrations. Clingempeel and colleagues placed both of these beliefs under the rubric of "nuclear family ideology." They contended that this ideology was responsible for some of the research limitations we identified earlier in this chapter: (a) minimal attention given to the structural complexity and heterogeneity of stepfamily forms, (b) emphasis on the problems and weaknesses of stepfamilies, rather than on potential strengths and advantages, and (c) general ignoring of the possibility that close relationships within remarried families may differ in fundamental ways from close relationships within nuclear families. Undoubtedly other nonepistemic values also have affected research on close relationships in remarried families.

Epistemic constraints that have influenced the shape of stepfamily literature include a bias toward between-group comparisons (comparing stepfamilies to other family structures), a disciplinary ethnocentric bias (ignoring the methods, perspectives, and theories of disciplines other than the one in which a researcher was trained), and the "rational objectivity" bias (Clingempeel, Flescher, & Brand, 1987). This last bias is a result of the belief that scientists should be objective and emotionally removed from their subjects; study participants are seen as passive objects to be examined, rather than as active coparticipants in the research endeavor (Thompson, 1992). The net effect of these epistemic constraints has been to limit the breadth, depth, and speed at which the body of knowledge on stepfamilies has been developed (Clingempeel, Flescher, & Brand, 1987).

Demographic Changes and the Development of the Field

The increased interest in remarried families among members of the scientific community came approximately 10 years after the rapid acceleration of the divorce rate. The increase in the divorce rate meant that many more American families than ever before experienced transitions from nuclear to single-parent or binuclear families. A majority of those individuals eventually made additional transitions into remarried families.

It became harder to ignore the remarried families resulting from the accelerated divorce rate in the 1960s and 1970s because, unlike the case of postbereavement, the stepparents in these postdivorce remarried families were additional, rather than substitute, parent figures (Wald, 1981). Remarriage postdivorce no longer closed the family circle and reconstituted the nuclear family; adding a stepparent postdivorce created new levels of kin and new interaction patterns. It also created issues that could not be ignored, stimulating new research and clinical practice.

When scholars began to explore the terrain of remarried family life, however, it was predominately with a nuclear family map. Because this map did not allow for a family to have more than two parents at a time, researchers, practitioners, and stepfamily members were forced to become pioneers in discovering the topography of this "brave new world."

2

Paths to Remarried Family Life

The various pathways to remarried family life have important implications for stepfamily dynamics. Obviously, remarried families do not begin with blank slates. Instead the individuals in remarried families are well into the process of writing their life stories when the remarriage relationships begin. The remarriage may start a new chapter, but the story lines continue from earlier chapters. Characters and events that were important in the development of earlier plots generally continue to influence the directions the stories take in later chapters.

The complexity of studying stepfamilies is magnified greatly when premarried family life is considered. Perhaps for this reason most researchers have tended to ignore the implications of these precursors to remarriage (Coleman & Ganong, 1990). Consequently, little is known about the effects of premarried family experiences on postremarriage relationships, other than what can be inferred from knowing certain structural characteristics of the remarried households and families being studied, such as whether one or both adults had children from prior relationships.

Some researchers, recognizing the potential influence of previous life experiences on remarried family functioning, have tried to control for these influences by limiting the types of stepfamilies in their samples. For example, samples often are restricted to postdivorce stepfather households only. The problem with this approach is the implicit assumption that previous life experiences, such as divorce, are discrete events with uniform effects on children and adults, an assumption that has been discredited by a growing body of research (Ahrons & Rodgers, 1987; Block, Block, & Gjerde, 1988). Moreover, sampling postdivorce stepfather households because they are more prevalent results in fewer studies of other stepfamilies (e.g., postbereavement stepfamilies, stepmother households). The assumption that close relationships in remarried families can be understood without knowing about the pre-remarriage relationship histories of both individuals is one that hampers progress in understanding stepfamily relationships.

Remarried families are formed in a number of ways. The pathway to remarriage written about most often by family researchers and clinicians is illustrated by the following scenario:

> Bob and Sue meet while in college and date for a few years before they marry. After a few years of marriage, they have children. When Bob Jr. is 15 and Sue Jr. is 12, Bob and Sue separate. Bob moves out of the family home, while Bob Jr. and Sue Jr. remain with Sue. After hostile divorce proceedings, Sue retains custody of the children and Bob is required to pay child support. Three years later, Bob remarries Linda, a divorced woman with a 6-year-old son. A year after that, Sue gets remarried to Alan, a man who has never been married before.

This scenario describes a first marriage that is ended by divorce as the precursor to two remarriages, one forming what is often called a *complex stepfamily* because both adults bring children to the remarried family (Bob and Linda), and the other creating a *simple stepfamily*, in which only one adult is a parent when the marriage begins (Sue and Alan). There are obviously other pathways to becoming a remarried family:

- A first marriage is ended by the death of a spouse.
- A single woman bears children, raises them alone for a while, and then marries a man who is not the father of the children.
- A single mother cohabits with, but does not marry, a man who is not the father of her children.
- A gay or lesbian person forms a committed partnership in which one or both have children from a prior relationship.

It should be noted that none of these pathways contain examples of remarriages, but all contain steprelationships, or de facto steprelationships.

It also should be noted that the examples cited above focus on second marriages or second relationships only; well over 10% of remarriages represent at least the third marriage for one or both of the partners (National Center for Health Statistics, 1993). An estimated 1 out of every 10 children will experience at least two divorces of their custodial parent before they turn 16 (Furstenberg, 1988). According to Bumpass (1984), 15% of children in remarried families will experience a second divorce within 2 years, and nearly 50% will experience one within 10 years. A sizable number of these children will become members of a second or third remarried family.

The family histories of "serial marriers" and their children are likely to be substantially different from those of stepfamily members who have experienced one prior marriage/committed relationship; unfortunately few researchers have examined the differences between those in their first remarriage and those who have had multiple marriages, so we can only speculate about the ways they might differ (Brody, Neubaum, & Forehand, 1988). At the very least, however, we know that the number of family transitions is greater for families in which adults have experienced a series of marriages or have cohabited a number of times. These transitions represent many potential changes for both adults and children, such as changing residences, the addition and loss of new household members, economic changes, and alterations in family identity.

To simplify the examination of the potential influences of prior history on remarried family life, we focus only on first remarriages in this chapter. Recognizing that we are oversimplifying things further by focusing on the prior experiences of only one of the adult partners, we briefly examine the potential differences in three types of preremarried families: postdivorce, postbereavement, and never-married.

❧ Postdivorce

Divorce is a verb, as well as a noun; a process that occurs over time, as well as a discrete legal event. Many people think only of the event, but the divorce process is what is most significant in shaping subsequent family dynamics and individual adjustment. The divorce process may extend over months or even years, and it is not unusual for one marital partner to have begun the psychological and emotional process of divorce well in advance of the other (Price & McKenry, 1988). We know of no research on how remarriage is affected by who decides to initiate the divorce, but research has been conducted on the differential effect of wanting/ not wanting divorce on the individual's adaptation to divorce (Price & McKenry, 1988). Thus it seems reasonable to propose that remarriage may be affected in some ways. For instance, the person who initiates the separation and divorce may be farther along in psychologically adjusting to divorce than is either the partner or the children, and consequently the initiator may be psychologically ready to enter another relationship earlier than are the children.

Although divorce is almost always a substantial disruption in people's lives, the divorce process does not have uniform psychological and emotional effects; some individuals welcome separation and divorce because the experience offers relief from family conflicts, physical or psychological abuse, and the psychopathological behaviors of certain family members, whereas others face divorcing with regret, sadness, and fear. It is probably fair to suggest that divorce is either an all positive or all negative process for only a few; for most there is an array of responses, including both relief and regret. We hypothesize that the functioning of close relationships in postdivorce remarried families is related to how individual family members thought about the divorce. Adults and children who welcomed divorce or who defined it as basically a "good thing" for themselves would be more likely to anticipate remarried family life with eagerness, as a chance for a new start, than those who defined divorce as basically a "bad thing." As of yet, the relation between the meaning of the divorce experience and subsequent close relationships in remarried families has not been examined empirically.

Postdivorce remarried families are typically the most complex because they are more likely than other remarried families to have both parents continue to be involved in raising the children. Stepparents in these situations become the third or perhaps fourth adult (when both parents remarry) involved in helping to raise children.

Connie Ahrons (1980) coined the term *binuclear* to refer to postdivorce families, implying that divorce creates two families with the same nucleus (the child). In these postdivorce binuclear families there are more adults, which means there are more relationships, and potentially a greater variety of personal relationships than in stepfamilies with other histories. In some postdivorce remarried families are types of relationships for which terms have not yet been invented. For example, consider the scenario presented earlier in this chapter. It has been suggested, only partly in jest, that the relationships between Bob and Alan and between Linda and Alan be referred to as "husband-in-law" and "wife-in-law," but this nomenclature has not been widely used, and these relationships remain nameless. Some have even facetiously referred to these persons as "outlaws."

Binuclear Families:
The Modern Extended Family?

Much of the family values rhetoric at the 1992 Republican National Convention was based on the common assumption that families used to be better than they are today. Goode (1963) referred to this assumption as "the world we have lost." The fact that this world never existed in the way it is believed to have existed does not seem to diminish the nostalgia in our society for strong, multiple-generation families living happily together under one roof (Coontz, 1992; Skolnick, 1991). Ironically the current families who most closely resemble the mythical extended families of the past are postdivorce binuclear families and stepfamilies.

From a longitudinal study of divorced parents, Ahrons (Ahrons & Rodgers, 1987) developed a typology of postdivorce binuclear families that has the potential to enlighten our understanding of remarried families. She referred to these five types as dissolved duos, perfect pals, cooperative colleagues, angry associates, and fiery foes.

Dissolved duos are the true single-parent families, those families in which former spouses have no contact after divorce. This is probably the largest group of postdivorce families. Furstenberg and Nord (1985), examining a nationally representative sample, found that fewer than half of children ages 11 to 17 years with divorced parents had seen their father the previous year, and almost 40% had had no contact with their father in 5 years or even knew where he was living.

The remarried families formed from dissolved duos are perhaps the most likely to live as reconstituted nuclear families. It is also relatively easy for the stepparents in these families to adopt the stepchildren and, consequently, for the family to legally join the ranks of nuclear families. Role definition problems are less salient in these families because the noncustodial biological parent is no longer in a parenting role. The stepparent in such a family often serves as a replacement or substitute parent. It is likely that relatives of the stepparent also substitute for the extended kin of the parent with whom there is no contact.

Perfect pals, although divorced, continue to have mutual respect for each other as people and as parents, and they remain good friends. Neither partner feels abandoned because there is a sense of mutuality about the divorce. Open, flexible boundaries are kept between the two households, and the shared parenting arrangements are of high quality. These couples often continue the rituals of the married family, such as sharing holidays and birthdays together with their children and maintaining relationships with each other's extended families.

From many perspectives the perfect pals have the ideal postdivorce relationship. The children do not have to contend with warring parents, and custody and child support issues are settled fairly and with minimal conflict. In Ahron's study, postdivorce couples who were perfect pals had remained single; it was difficult for each individual to develop an independent lifestyle.

We hypothesize that the stepparent entering remarriage with a postdivorce perfect pal might feel quite threatened by the continued intimacy maintained by the divorced couple. Finding roles within the new stepfamily could be extremely difficult. The open, flexible boundaries maintained by the divorced couple that worked well when they were single might feel like an invasion of privacy to the new spouse. The new spouse also may be less than enthusiastic about spending holidays with their spouse's ex-spouse and the stepchildren! Additionally, any changes in routines and family rituals brought about by the remarriage—for example, holiday celebrations—might be resented by the children. Conflicts and jealousy are likely to occur between the biological parent and the stepparent (between father and stepfather or between mother and stepmother), and loyalty conflicts for the children may be quite common as well.

Cooperative colleagues would not describe themselves as good friends, but they are able to cooperate well as parents. These couples make compromises for the sake of the children and do not let conflicts escalate into huge power struggles. This type of postdivorce relationship may be the most functional pathway to remarriage. Giles-Sims (1987a) found that positive contact between the ex-spouses was associated with cohesion, expressiveness, and lack of conflict in stepfamilies. The children's needs are met because the parents are able to put their differences aside for the sake of the children, yet clear boundaries are drawn between each parent's role as coparent and the role as ex-spouse. The ex-spouse relationship of cooperative colleagues is likely to be less intrusive in the remarriage than is true in the case of perfect pals. It may be, however, that some children have a more difficult time determining unique roles for stepparents when parents are so cooperative with each other. Clinicians have argued that children fantasize about their divorced parents reuniting (Sager et al., 1983; Visher & Visher, 1988; Wald, 1981); this imaging may be especially true when children see parents who are perfect pals or cooperative colleagues.

Angry associates still have bitter, resentful feelings about the past marriage, as well as the divorce process. Their anger with each other is still an integral part of their divorced relationship. These couples tend to parallel parent, rather than coparent. Typically the mother has control of the children, and the father has control of the money. The mother often "punishes" the father by not allowing him access to the children, and the father retaliates by withholding child support or vice versa. The children get caught in the middle and tend to express ongoing loyalty conflicts. Remarriage by either ex-spouse is likely to exacerbate the hostility.

Because of loyalty conflicts on the part of the children and poor parenting communication between the ex-spouses who are angry associates, dynamics within the stepfamily often may be difficult. Planning for holidays and vacations is frequently traumatic. Stepparents may feel that their lives are being controlled by people they do not like or may not even know (the ex-spouse of their spouse). These difficult dynamics probably contribute to the high divorce rate among remarried families with children (White & Booth, 1985). Sometimes stepparents can help by serving as a neutral go-between for the children, but they also may team up with their spouse in the continuing battle with the ex-spouse. Jealousies among the adults make it difficult for children to establish positive relationships with all of the parents (Crosbie-Burnett, 1984).

An even worse scenario is played out by *fiery foes*. These couples have almost no ability to coparent. Their anger is so intense that they cannot accept each other's parenting rights. The other parent is the enemy! Every attempt is made to remove the ex-spouse from the lives of the children. These couples still are very attached to each other, though they would deny it. The children are caught in the middle and often take sides with one parent or the other. Among these couples, one parent, usually the father, sees the children less and less frequently over the years. Both parents blame each other for this decline, and the children become pawns in the continuing battle.

It is difficult for a stepparent to enter such a volatile situation. The noncustodial parent may say damaging things to the children about the stepparent as a means of upsetting the ex-spouse. These efforts, in turn, may make it difficult for the stepparent-stepchild relationship to evolve positively. The stepparent also may come to resent the amount of emotional energy the spouse spends on maintaining the battles with the ex-spouse.

❧ Postbereavement

Postbereavement remarried families have quite different experiences from those of the previously divorced. The hostility of the fiery foes and the angry associates does not permeate these families, but neither are there the opportunities for sharing and the divisions of labor characteristic of perfect pals or cooperative colleagues.

Custody issues, a major source of contention for some postdivorce stepfamilies, are unlikely to be a problem for postbereavement families. The feelings of children torn between divorced parents who have legal custody rights and who interact with the children regularly are likely to be different from the torn loyalties that children feel when one parent is deceased. In stepfamilies formed after parental divorce, children may be torn between feelings for both parents or between feelings for a parent and a stepparent. After the death of a parent, loyalty conflicts may be more likely to be experienced by a child wondering whether he or she can be close to a stepparent and still honor the memory of a deceased parent. Clinicians advise that it is important for children to be allowed to mourn their deceased parent and to be given the freedom to define the role of a stepparent as something other than the parent's replacement (Visher & Visher, 1988). We have talked to many middle-aged adults who remain bitterly resentful of being forced as a child to refer to their stepparent as Mom or Dad.

The levels of social support provided for the head of a single-parent household may differ considerably, depending on gender and the circumstances that led to single-parent status (Furstenberg & Cherlin, 1991; McKenry & Price, 1991). On the one hand, some divorced parents may receive less support from their kin and very little, if any, support from their former in-laws. On the other hand, widowed single parents are likely to receive a great deal of social support from their own kin, as well as the kin of the deceased spouse (Lopata, 1979).

Empirical studies provide little guidance for members of step-families formed postbereavement, and guidance from clinical and self-help literature is limited as well. Ironically, works of fiction may provide the most insight into the issues facing the members of postbereavement remarried families (Coleman & Ganong, 1986a).

❧ Never-Married Parents

Although they are increasingly common, little is known about stepfamilies formed when a previously unmarried parent (usually the mother) brings a child to the new relationship. Filinson (1986) labeled these relationships "de facto stepfamilies" and suggested that due to the increase in cohabitation and childbearing outside of marriage, it is no longer justified to confine the study of step-families to only those constituted legally through remarriage.

De facto stepfamilies are of two basic types. One is formed when the adults legally marry. Because these families contain a first marriage and stepparent-stepchild relationships, they fall some-where between a nuclear family and a stepfamily. We hypothesize that most "choose" to emulate nuclear families and to assume that identity. Of all types of remarried families, these are probably the most likely to function as a nuclear family and to think of them-selves as a nuclear family unit, particularly when the biological father has had no contact. In fact, Filinson (1986), using data from a study of the family lives of children born outside of legal mar-riage in Great Britain, found that at least half of the children living in these stepfamilies were unaware that the father in the family was a stepfather (though the father was aware that the child was a stepchild). These families probably do not identify themselves to researchers as stepfamilies; children think of the stepparents as their parents, and they address them as such. Partly because of this invisibility, information about these remarried families is limited.

The other category of remarried families contains those that cohabit but never marry. These families usually are categorized by

demographers as single-parent families, and they do not get counted
when legal marriages only are used to define remarried families.
Because they are unlikely to define themselves to researchers as
members of a remarried family, data about people in these relationships are hard to obtain. The adults who form these families
are probably the least conventional of any of the groups discussed
in this chapter. They likely receive the least amount of formal and
informal social support, they are the most stigmatized, and they
probably are generally poorer than families in the other categories. In short, if remarried families in general are not supported
by societal guidelines, norms, and institutions (Cherlin, 1978),
then these families, the least institutionalized group of remarried
families, are also the least supported of all remarried families.
Consequently, we hypothesize that they will be less stable.

It is important to keep in mind that positive and negative life
events are not randomly distributed among these pathways. For
instance, the life experiences of widows and divorcees who remarry are likely to differ. An adult whose spouse voluntarily left
him or her (e.g., divorce) may feel devastated. In the case of
women, they may remarry to obtain financial security for their
children and themselves (Folk, Graham, & Beller, 1992). If their
self-esteem has been damaged seriously by the divorce, they may
not wisely choose a new spouse. When a partner dies, the spouse
may be devastated; however, his or her self-esteem is less likely to
suffer. When a marriage is ended through death, there is less likely
to have been a legacy of hostility and acrimony to overcome than
when divorce occurs. Relationships ended by death may also
provide a sense of closure or finality that never occurs in the
divorce process. The ambiguity of incomplete closure following
divorce may be more difficult for some individuals to cope with
than the certainty of death.

ઋ Who Remarries?
A Profile of Remarriages

The following descriptions of who remarries are based on legal
remarriages, so de facto (cohabiting) remarriages are excluded.

These demographic profiles generally include both remarriages of those with children and those without; keep in mind that not all of these remarriages will create stepfamilies.

Remarriage After Divorce

The *number* of postdivorce remarriages is increasing, but the *rate* of postdivorce remarriages is declining slightly. The number is increasing because a larger number of divorced people are eligible for remarriage. The slight decrease in the rate of remarriage is likely due to an avoidance by some of legal repartnerships (Wilson & Clarke, 1992). Divorced people may be reluctant to enter another legal marriage contract because of unpleasant experiences related to the dissolution of their marriages. Many people do not realize when they first marry that they are entering into a legal contract with their partner, one in which the state has a vested interest. They often realize this only when they attempt to dissolve the contract through divorce. Despite the advent, two decades ago, of so-called no-fault dissolution of marriage, the legal process of divorce still can be an emotionally and financially wrenching experience that many persons would rather not repeat.

Income. The stereotype is that men take a financial beating in divorce, but the reality is that women (and children) are the ones who generally lose economically after divorce (Hoffman & Duncan, 1988). Consequently the financial motivation to remarry is greater for women than for men; per capita income of females decreases substantially after divorce and increases after remarriage, but for men the opposite pattern ensues (Day & Bahr, 1986). The remarriage rate for women who are financially secure, securely employed, and well educated is lower than for women who are financially insecure (Oh, 1986). This finding suggests that economic survival may be an impetus for many women to remarry. In fact, for divorced women the surest way to escape poverty is to remarry (Folk et al., 1992).

Age. Remarriage rates decline with age for both men and women. Divorced men remarry at a higher rate than divorced women for every age group except those ages 20 to 24 (Wilson & Clarke, 1992). The average age for divorced men at remarriage in 1988 was 38.6 years, and for women it was 35 years. Remarriers are thus about 10 to 12 years older, on average, than those marrying for the first time.

Time Since Divorce. The interval between marriages is fairly short. On average, both men and women remarry within 4 years of their divorce; the interval between marriages increases as people get older (Wilson & Clarke, 1992). Men remarry more rapidly than women, and whites remarry more rapidly than blacks or other racial groups (Wilson & Clarke, 1992). Almost 30% of divorced persons remarry within 12 months of their divorce, indicating that they have very short courtships or that many knew their future partners before they were divorced (Wilson & Clarke, 1992). These remarried courtships may be even shorter than it appears from the vital statistics because the majority of remarried couples live together prior to legally remarrying (Ganong & Coleman, 1989; Hanna & Knaub, 1984; Montgomery, Anderson, Hetherington, & Clingempeel, 1992).

New Partner's Marital Status. The majority (61%) of divorced men and women remarry other divorced people, 35% marry single men and women, and 4% marry widowed individuals (Wilson & Clarke, 1992). The previous marital status of the new partners of divorced persons is related to the divorced person's age: Those under 30 are more likely to marry never-married persons, those 30 to 64 are more likely to marry divorced partners, and after age 45 the proportion marrying previously divorced persons decreases and marriages to widows and widowers increase.

Race. Whites are more likely to remarry than other racial groups, and blacks are the least likely to remarry (Bumpass, Sweet, & Castro Martin, 1990; Smock, 1990; Wilson & Clarke, 1992). Blacks are more likely to separate without divorcing, to stay single for longer periods of time after divorce, and to remarry less frequently than whites. The effects of other variables on remarriage probability (e.g., number of children, education level) sometimes vary substantially for blacks and whites (Koo, Suchindran, & Griffith, 1984; Smock, 1990).

Children From Previous Relationships. It has been hypothesized that children represent costs to potential remarriage partners that serve to lower the probability of remarriage for parents (Becker, Landis, & Michael, 1977). Some research supports this hypothesis (Becker et al., 1977; Bumpass et al., 1990), but other demographic studies have not found a relation between children and remarriage probability, or they have found that children are a deterrent to remarriage only for younger women (cf. Koo & Suchindran, 1980).

Gender. There are gender differences in remarriage after divorce. Men remarry more quickly and at a higher rate than women. In general, divorced women who are older (Wilson & Clarke, 1992), who are highly educated, and who are occupationally and financially independent are less likely to remarry (Bumpass et al., 1990; Oh, 1986). For men, the opposite pattern is generally true.

Remarriage After Widowhood

The number of widowed men and women remarrying has dropped and is only about 10% of the number of divorced men and women who remarry (Wilson & Clarke, 1992). As with the divorced, increased cohabitation probably explains part of the reduction in the remarriage rate (Wilson & Clarke, 1992). Finances also probably play a role in cohabitation decisions for the widowed; insurance or social security benefits may be lost if people remarry.

Income. Widowhood lowers economic well-being, and remarriage substantially improves economic well-being for both men and women. But women benefit more (Zick & Smith, 1988). This finding leads one to think that the widowed seek new partners for economic stability. However, widowed people who remarry are better off financially even before they remarry than the widowed who do not remarry (Zick & Smith, 1988). For widows over age 60, education and remarriage rates are inversely related (K. Smith,

Zick, & Duncan, 1991), but for widowers over age 60, the more education they have, the greater the likelihood they will remarry. Higher levels of financial security appear to have an insignificant effect on the likelihood of remarriage for widows and widowers (K. Smith et al., 1991).

Age. Widowed grooms in 1988 averaged 60.9 years, and widowed brides had a mean age of 53.1 years (Wilson & Clarke, 1992). As widowed people get older, the likelihood they will remarry decreases; widows' chances diminish more than those of widowers.

Time Since Bereavement. The mean interval between marriages for widowed men is similar to that for divorced people, except after age 35, when widowers actually remarry more rapidly than divorced men. Widowed women have a longer period of time between marriages than do widowed men or divorced men and women (Wilson & Clarke, 1992).

New Partner's Marital Status. Men and women remarry widowed and divorced persons in approximately equal proportions, although younger widows and widowers are more likely to remarry divorced persons, and older individuals are more likely to remarry others who were widowed (Wilson & Clarke, 1992). For men, the previous marital status of their remarriage partner is not related to the interval between marriages. For women, widows who marry single men marry the soonest; those who remarry widowed men remain single the longest.

Race. Blacks have longer intervals between marriages than whites even though black widowed persons are younger on average than whites. Blacks are less likely than whites to remarry after widowhood (K. Smith et al., 1991). It has long been believed that many of these differences were due to greater cohabitation by blacks than whites, but Bumpass and Sweet (1989) found no evidence to support higher cohabitation rates for nonwhites.

Children From Previous Relationships. Children serve as a deterrent to remarriage for middle-aged widowed men and women (K. Smith et al., 1991). Presumably no one has looked at this question for older widowed persons, perhaps because the assumption is that "children" of the elderly widowed are middle-aged adults themselves and are less likely to play a role in decisions to remarry.

Gender. For both middle-aged and older widowed persons, men are far more likely to remarry than women (K. Smith et al., 1991). Men are less likely to outlive a spouse than women but are more likely to remarry if they do.

It should be clear from what has been said in this chapter that there is no single pathway to remarriage and that, increasingly, people are choosing not to remarry at all. However, a number of factors have been identified that tend to push people along the remarriage pathway. Collins (1991) argued that the decision to set up a home with another adult is brought about by a combination of private, personal pressures and pressures relating to wider social processes.

As we have noted, women often are driven to remarriage as a means of overcoming poverty or, at the very least, a postdivorce lowered standard of living (Weitzman, 1988). They may be demoralized by their children's complaints of unfulfilled material needs and may seek relief through remarriage. Mothers also may be extremely sensitive to the negative attributes that society ascribes to the children of mother-headed single-parent households.

Collins (1991) even indicated:

> There is a tendency for minority arrangements like lone-parent families to be seen as something of an affront to established beliefs about family life. If such families can be seen to "work," they undermine the credibility of the nuclear family, and this has subversive implications for the dominant economic and moral order which to a great extent depends on the nuclear family and in its turn endorses it. (p. 159)

Collins goes on to say, "This creates a climate of blame which many lone parents experience as a pressure to regularize their lives and to create a 'proper' two-parent home for their children" (p. 160).

Fathers who have custody of their children may feel especially pressured to create a "proper" home for their children by providing them with an "*en site* mother." Mothers of older children, especially boys, may feel the need for a partner to help with the discipline.

Other explanations for individuals choosing the path to remarriage include the societal push to view being romantically in love and having this love reciprocated as a major goal in life (Goetting, 1982). This goal may seem especially appealing to the partner who did not instigate his or her divorce—the "left," rather than the "leaver." Others seek remarriage partners because they are lonely; still others choose remarriage to alleviate the feelings of failure often brought about by divorce. Some view marriage as more "normal" than being divorced and are eager to leave behind their more truncated social life of singlehood for the perceived fuller and more normal social life available to married couples (Goetting, 1982).

There are numerous other reasons why individuals remarry. In fact, each person may have a completely individualized set of reasons evolving from his or her unique experiences in previous marriages, coupled with his or her experiences in singlehood. Ironically, in terms of public attitudes and the ideologies underlying them, people choosing remarriage may be going from the frying pan into the fire (Collins, 1991). Remarriage is seldom the same as first marriage: The single parent may remarry only to find that he or she has replaced one challenging family situation with the new, even more complex and challenging stepfamily.

3

Remarriage Relationships

The remarriage relationship is an important one in remarried families. After all, the remarried family is created because two adults decide to form a partnership, so it is logical to expect that partnership to be a critical element of the remarried family. In traditional family systems theory the married partners are considered to be the architects of the family, the foundation on which the family is built (Satir, 1972). Although this position has been challenged by those who think the stepparent-stepchild relationship is the pivotal relationship in remarried families (Crosbie-Burnett, 1984; Mills, 1984), agreement is widespread that remarried couple relationships are extremely important for the well-being of both the adult partners and other family members.

In Chapter 2 we provide a brief demographic overview of who remarries. In this chapter we examine research and theory on (a) remarriage courtship, (b) the stability and quality of remarriages compared to first marriages, and (c) some aspects of remarriage dynamics (e.g., communication, power). We begin by examining how the courtship process in remarriage differs from that of first marriages. Then we examine remarriage courtship behaviors; to understand remarriage relationships, it is important to understand the courtship process. Cate and Lloyd (1992) argued persuasively that courtship processes set the foundation for later marital stability and satisfaction.

❧ Courtship for Remarriage

Americans are smitten with the institution of marriage. The United States has one of the highest marriage rates in the world (Cate & Lloyd, 1992). Some social commentators decry the relatively high rates of divorce in the United States as an indication that marriage is a dying institution. Others point to the fact that 75% of those who divorce eventually remarry, an indication that people may be rejecting specific partners but still are attracted to the cultural institution of marriage (Bumpass et al., 1990).

Dr. Samuel Johnson, the 18th-century English author, philosopher, and social critic, allegedly once wrote that remarriage is the triumph of hope over experience. Apparently Americans are full of hope, because we have one of the highest rates of remarriage in the world (Ishii-Kuntz & Coltrane, 1992). In fact, half of all marriages in the United States involve at least one previously married partner (Bumpass et al., 1990).

Despite remarriage being a widespread phenomenon, most research on courtship has focused on young people who have never been married (Cate & Lloyd, 1992; Rodgers & Conrad, 1986). Some of what is known about mate selection for first marriages can be generalized to remarital courtship. However, substantial differences are also likely between the two because of the number of differences between those who have been married and those who have not.

Courtship Differences
Between First Marriages and Remarriages

Age. One potential difference is age; those who remarry are nearly a decade older, on average, than those who marry for the first time. In mate selection, age is a proxy variable representing several other characteristics of individuals, such as life experiences, expectations, and lifestyle choices. Older people bring more to courtship; in general they have done more, known more people, and had a broader range of experiences. Their expectations for what they want in a partner may have changed, they have established a lifestyle, and they have expressed preferences in leisure time activities, religion, and careers. In short, older adults generally have a more complete sense of self than younger adults. Consequently they are more likely than younger, never-married people to have made some choices about their lives that should make a difference in whom they choose and how they choose a mate.

A demographic consequence of the older age of formerly married persons seeking mates is that as people get older, there are fewer potentially eligible partners. The situation is especially difficult for women because the male-to-female ratio increasingly favors men with each older age group. To compound the problem, men tend to choose younger partners and women tend to choose older partners, thus further reducing the number of eligible partners for women as they age. This reduced pool of eligible partners probably has a number of effects on courtship behavior. It may encourage hasty choices and facilitate making decisions about partners on the belief that "a bird in the hand is worth two in the bush." In some ways the intrapersonal advantages of aging, such as knowing oneself better, are offset by the restricted choice of partners, especially for women.

Marital Experience. An obvious difference between remarriage courtship and first-marriage courtship is that those who are seeking a remarital partner have been through the courtship process at least once and have had the experience of establishing a household with someone else. They potentially have learned through experience what they want and do not want within a marriage. This firsthand knowledge and marital experience may very well have an impact on how these people look for future partners and/or what partner characteristics they seek.

The *training ground perspective* of remarriage holds that first marriages serve as a learning experience that influences the type of person chosen for subsequent marriages. Presumably some people seek partners who are quite different from their previous mate, particularly if they believe that characteristics of their former partner contributed to their marital problems. Other individuals may believe that they understand themselves better as a result of the previous marriage and thus seek mates who are compatible with the individual's true self. Regardless of the lessons learned from prior marriages, the courtship of previously married persons is likely to be different from the courtship of those without prior marriage experience.

Children. A substantial difference between remarriage courtship and the courtship of most young, never-married persons can be the presence of children. Parents, particularly those whose children reside with them, probably have less time to spend in courtship-related activities such as dating. They may be so busy earning a living and raising children that courtship behaviors are low priorities for them. Parents also may have different criteria for future partners than do nonparents. For example, they may be seeking someone who they believe would be a good coparent as well as a spouse.

As we note in Chapter 2, some demographers and other social science researchers who use social exchange models of mate selection have postulated that children represent costs that presumably make finding a partner more difficult and lower the mothers' probability of remarriage (Becker et al., 1977). However, it is also possible that children represent benefits to some prospective partners; gaining an instant family is appealing to some men and women. Having children also may increase some individuals' motivation to find a partner, thus accelerating search behaviors.

These hypotheses are speculative, however, because we do not know under what conditions children serve either as motivation or deterrent to remarriage. In fact, researchers seldom have examined how children fit into the courtship process (a study by Montgomery et al., 1992, is an exception). Clinicians generally advise parents to include their children in the later stages of the courtship process, after parents and prospective partners have become serious about their relationship (Walker & Messinger, 1979). The assumption is that this inclusion in courtship will facilitate bonding between children and their future stepparent, but whether this actually occurs is not known. In fact, very little is known about how and when single parents involve their children in courtship activities.

Remarriage Courtship Behaviors

We do know some things about remarriage courtship. Remarriers court for brief periods of time, they do little to prepare for remarriage, they tend to live together before marriage, and their reasons for marriage tend to be pragmatic. We also know that gender differences exist in remarriage courtship behaviors and that remarriers are more likely than first marriers to wed someone who is different from themselves. What follows is a brief overview of what is known and what needs to be learned about courtship for remarriage.

Length of Courtship. Research data on the length of time between relationships should be considered only as estimates, at least for those who remarry postdivorce. Most calculations are based on the period between the final divorce and the legal remarriage. However, many people begin dating after they are separated but before they are divorced, and many remarried couples cohabit prior to legally remarrying (Ganong & Coleman, 1989; Hanna & Knaub, 1984; Montgomery et al., 1992). Although Montgomery and colleagues found a tremendous diversity in the patterns of courtship, it is safe to conclude that for most remarriers the courtship period is relatively short. For example, O'Flaherty and Eells (1988) found that a sample of remarried Catholics courted a median of 9 months, nearly half the time spent in their first-marriage courting period. In the Virginia Longitudinal Study of Divorce and Remarriage, 80% of the remarried women dated their future spouses for 1 year or less before cohabiting, and for more than a third, the period was 3 months or less (Montgomery et al., 1992). Older remarriers (over age 60) also tend to have short courtships; Vinick (1978) found that more than half of the 24 elderly remarried couples she interviewed married within a year of starting their relationships.

Does the length of courtship affect subsequent family relationships? Rodgers and Conrad (1986) hypothesized that shorter time periods between divorce and remarriage would enhance remarried family relationships. They reasoned that remarriage would be less disruptive if postdivorce families had not had time to develop new patterns of interaction and new family rituals. It is equally plausible to hypothesize the opposite relation; namely, that rapidly occurring multiple family transitions would be detrimental to family relationships. However, in the only study in which this relation was examined, the length of courtship had no connection to remarried family relationships (Montgomery et al., 1992).

Remarriers appear to make relatively quick decisions about future partners. It is unknown whether this rapidity is because (a) they have a clear idea of what they want in a relationship and when they find a person with the qualities they seek, they "go for it," or (b) whether, because opportunities are few, they settle quickly when any potential partner appears. Ambert (1989), in a longitudinal study, found that multidivorced persons remarried much more quickly and after a shorter acquaintance than the once-divorced. She concluded that getting married per se was important to the multidivorced, whereas getting married to the right partner was the goal of the once-divorced.

Preparation for Remarriage. Given the relatively short courting periods, it is not surprising that remarried couples do little to prepare for remarriage (Ganong & Coleman, 1989; Hanna & Knaub, 1984). Less than 25% of the 105 remarried families in a study we conducted sought remarriage counseling, attended support groups or educational offerings designed to prepare people for life in stepfamilies, or discussed their pending remarriage with friends. Less than half read self-help books and magazine articles about remarriage and stepparenting (Ganong & Coleman, 1989). Hanna and Knaub (1984) found a similar lack of preparation in a group of remarried couples, and clinicians have reported the difficulty of getting stepparents and their spouses to attend workshops and educational programs, both before and after remarriage (Pill, 1981).

Apparently the primary way people prepare for remarriage is to live together prior to legally remarrying. Although this preparation technique may have intuitive appeal, there is little evidence that it is effective. In our study, couples who cohabited did not discuss stepfamily issues anymore frequently than those who did not cohabit.

The lack of purposeful planning for remarriage is puzzling, particularly in light of the generally pessimistic cultural images held regarding remarried family relationships. It would seem that adults entering a remarriage would make extra efforts to prepare themselves. Why do they not? Several reasons are possible. First, the attitude that "if it isn't broken, don't fix it" is a pervasive perspective that discourages problem prevention. Our society is not generally oriented to preventing problems before they occur, and couples contemplating remarriage are probably no exception. Second, couples planning remarriage may be oblivious to anything but their own joy and excitement, a form of tunnel vision that prevents them from seeing potential problems that could be avoided by pre-remarriage planning. Also remarried couples simply might be naive about what to expect and thus feel little need for preparation. In our study the majority of adults had positive expectations for remarriage and steprelationships, suggesting that they viewed formal preparation as unnecessary. Third, there may be an absence of well-qualified assistance for remarriage and stepfamily preparation. Stepfamily self-help groups may not be available, couples may not have access to counselors and clergy who are trained in understanding the dynamics of remarried family life, and helpful reading material may not be accessible.

Obviously, couples who are remarrying talk with each other as part of their courtship, but their conversations may not cover issues deemed important by stepfamily clinicians. In our study, only about half of the couples discussed children from prior relationships, less than a fourth discussed finances, and no other specific topic was discussed by more than 15% of the couples (Ganong & Coleman, 1989). It is highly probable that hope for a bright future together, coupled with an absence of extreme, overt problems, motivated these couples to avoid delving too deeply into potential difficulties. "Leave well enough alone" may be the motto of many remarrying couples, a stance that hinders them from working to prevent problems before they arise. This *avoidance hypothesis* may be the best explanation for not preparing for remarriage. Whatever the reason, it is an unfortunate phenomenon because clinicians assert that the majority of problems confronting stepfamilies, apart from individual problems such as alcoholism and personality disorders, are preventable (Sager et al., 1983; Visher & Visher, 1988).

Cohabitation. A majority of those who remarry live together prior to legally marrying (Bumpass, 1990). For other couples, cohabiting is an alternative, and not a prelude, to legal remarriage. Those who never legally remarry may wish to avoid becoming involved in legal entanglements, may be afraid of making the commitments they believe to be inherent in legal unions, or may not philosophically agree with the institution of marriage.

For those who cohabit as part of the remarriage courtship process, cohabiting may be an attempt to assess compatibility and to get to know one another via daily interaction. It also could be that dating is uncomfortable for older adults. Their social scripts for dating may be decades old, which makes them feel foolish and uncertain about what to do. The social norms for dating are aimed generally at young, never-married, childless individuals. Although a number of self-help organizations and entrepreneurial dating services have attempted to make dating easier for middle-aged and older adults, formerly married persons, especially those who had been married for many years, may be more comfortable setting up housekeeping with a partner than dating. Combining two households is seldom easy, but for some it may be a simpler alternative than contending with the ambiguities of dating.

What is the process of cohabiting? Montgomery and colleagues (1992) reported that some remarried mothers in their study *partially cohabited* for a period of weeks or months before fully merging households. This finding meant that the prospective male partner spent a few days and nights per week in the mother's household for a time before he moved in and resided with his future wife and stepchildren on a full-time basis. Aside from this study, little is known about the process of cohabitation prior to remarriage. Given the pervasiveness of cohabiting as either a prelude to or an alternative to legal remarriage, it is surprising that so little is known about the process by which couples decide to live together, how children are informed, and the effects on the entire stepfamily system.

Reasons to Remarry. Some researchers have found that the previously married have more pragmatic than romantic motivations to marry (Farrell & Markman, 1986; Ganong & Coleman, 1989; Kvanli & Jennings, 1987; Vinick, 1978). Among the pragmatic reasons for remarriage are financial security, help in raising children, response to social pressure, response to legal threats regarding the custody of children, relief from loneliness, the need for a regular sexual partner, pregnancy, the need to have someone to take care of, the need to be taken care of, and convenience. These practical reasons help explain the short courtships of some remarried couples, as well as the tendency for partners to cohabit prior to remarriage. Certainly these are not the only reasons; love, a desire for companionship, shared interests, and liking the partner are also common reasons why people remarry.

The generally more pragmatic reasons for remarriage suggest one of two primary influences on courtship behaviors. First, it could be that those who are in the remarriage market know what they want and need; their courtship search is not blinded by thoughts of finding their one true love, but rather is guided by more purposeful considerations. Second, it could be that those in the remarriage market are desperate for help (e.g., financial, child rearing) and may feel pressured to find somebody willing to mate with them. Thus the formerly married may make bad choices based on immediate, pressing needs.

Gender Differences in Courtship. What are some logical reasons to expect gender differences in remarriage courtship behaviors? The so-called *marriage gradient,* in which men are expected to be older, taller, better educated, and more financially successful than their female partners, may be relevant in explaining gender differences in remarriage mate selection. Jesse Bernard (1972), a pioneering feminist sociologist, reported more than two decades ago that the adults least likely to marry were men who had little education and low incomes, and women who had much education and high incomes, a phenomenon she attributed, in part, to the marriage gradient norm. Although evidence shows that relationships are becoming more egalitarian, the marriage gradient as a social norm is also still in operation (Ganong & Coleman, 1992).

From demographic data (see Chapter 2) we know that men are more likely than women to remarry and that they remarry more rapidly than women. We also know that well-educated and financially secure women are less likely than other women to remarry but that the opposite holds true for men. Women are more likely then men to have physical and legal custody of children after divorce, and women are more likely than men to be widowed.

These differences suggest that the opportunities to remarry are not the same for women as they are for men. They also suggest that men and women have different economic, emotional, and familial motivations to remarry. Bernard (1972) pointed out that every marriage is really two marriages—his and hers—and that his marriage is a lot better emotionally, physically, socially, and financially than hers. Therefore, previously married women, whether they wanted their marriage to end or not, may be less enthusiastic than men about recontracting a marriage. Walker and Messinger (1979) observed that women may be reluctant to give up the autonomy and personal freedom they enjoy as single adults to enter another union; however, this finding may be true primarily for women who are financially secure.

Ambert (1983), in a qualitative, longitudinal study of divorced and remarried families, found that the courtship behaviors of financially secure women differed from those of financially insecure women. Women with financial means exercised a higher degree of choice in the men they dated, had more opportunities for dates, met more men, and had more steady relationships than women with limited finances. Yet women with means were also more selective in their dating choices and more often rejected relationships. Financially secure women also were less often exploited, manipulated, or abused by the men they dated. In general, women who had economic resources less often planned to be married in the future.

In Remarriages, Opposites Attract. For the most part remarried couples are less similar to each other on demographic characteristics (e.g., age, education, religion) than first-married couples (Dean & Gurak, 1978). Three explanations have been offered for these differences: (a) They may be due to divorced persons purposefully choosing someone different from their first partners, who may have been demographically similar to themselves, (b) they may be a result of the reduced choices of partners available in the marriage market (the smaller pool of people to choose from increases the odds that partners will be less similar to each other in remarriage), and (c) it may be that some people are predisposed to "bad" marital choices, tending to choose partners who are more different from themselves than they are similar. In a study designed to examine and compare these perspectives, it was found that remarried women may be prone to making bad marital choices: (a) The first marriage partners of remarried women are less similar to themselves than are the partners of women still in their first marriages, and (b) the second partners of remarried women are even more different from them than were their first husbands (Dean & Gurak, 1978).

In the next section we look at the impact of partner similarity and other characteristics of individuals and couples on the stability and quality of remarriages. Interest in these topics is great because remarriages are more fragile relationships than first marriages.

❧ Remarriage Stability and Quality

The divorce rate for remarriages is slightly higher than for first marriages (Castro Martin & Bumpass, 1989). A number of explanations have been proposed to account for the greater fragility of remarriages. Explanatory models include intraindividual, interpersonal, and societal-level factors as causal influences. Generally the same explanatory models have been proposed in studies of the satisfaction, adjustment, and quality of remarriages. Complex phenomena such as remarriage satisfaction and stability usually have multiple, simultaneously occurring causes. We present these explanations separately, however, because that is how most scholars have proposed and tested them and because it is easier to present them one at a time. We describe each of these explanations for remarriage instability and remarriage quality and present evidence to support or refute them.

Intraindividual Causes
for Remarital Instability

Divorce Proneness. The *divorce-prone personality hypothesis* proposes differences in personality between those who stay married to one partner and those who divorce and remarry. According to this perspective, remarriages contain an overrepresentation of individuals who are poor marriage material; their personalities make it likely that their marriages will be unstable. Personality characteristics such as low frustration tolerance, impulsivity, risk taking, alcohol and drug abuse, and antisocial behaviors have been proposed as the kinds of factors that negatively affect marital quality and stability (McCranie & Kahan, 1986).

Although the divorce-prone personality hypothesis is an intraindividual explanation for redivorce, societal-level factors contribute to making this a plausible explanation. First, as we mentioned earlier in this chapter, remarriage preparation is not a norm in our culture, so those with personalities and temperaments that might make marriage more difficult are not likely to get preventive counseling or advice. Second, in the United States it is the norm for adults to be married, and social pressure is exerted on those who willingly deviate from this norm (Goetting, 1982). Thus people remarry because it is easier and more socially acceptable to be married than to be single. The social pressure to be married is democratic; it is applied regardless of how temperamentally well suited individuals are to be married and how emotionally stable they are. Although the social pressure to be married and the stigma of divorce and unmarried parenthood have diminished in recent years, the cultural attitudes are still such that being married is seen as the most desirable state, especially for parents (Ganong, Coleman, & Mapes, 1990; Gerstel, 1987).

The divorce-prone personality hypothesis, in particular, has been used to explain the behaviors of *serial marriers*, those who marry three or more times (Brody et al., 1988; Counts, 1992). In a prospective study McCranie and Kahan (1986) found that male physicians who had been divorced more than once had different MMPI profiles from those physicians who did not have multiple divorces, indicating that they were less conformist, more impulsive, more extroverted, and more risk taking. In addition the multiply divorced men reported engaging in negative health practices more often than men with other marital histories, which the authors interpreted as reflecting a less structured, more risk-taking lifestyle (McCranie & Kahan, 1986).

In another longitudinal study, support for the divorce-prone personality hypothesis was found only for women (Kurdek, 1990). Remarried wives who had been divorced more than once reported more anxiety, phobias, paranoid ideation, psychoticism, and general distress than those in first marriages and those in first remarriages (divorced only once). However, the data did not allow for drawing causal inferences about the direction of effects between personality and marital satisfaction; it is also possible that multiple divorces caused the women to be more distressed. Finally, Booth and Edwards (1992) found only weak support for a connection between personality characteristics and divorce risk in remarriages for men and women.

Despite the limited empirical support for the divorce-prone personality hypothesis, we expect it to generate more research in the future. The notion that some people are not well suited for marriage because of personality or temperamental predispositions has intuitive appeal, and a sizeable body of research relates personality and marital satisfaction in first marriages.

Future research should not be limited to examining only the effects of extreme or deviant personality traits. Researchers should expand their studies to include the effects of personality traits that may not be pathological per se but that still may predispose individuals to cope either poorly or well with the unique demands of stepfamily living. For instance, Clingempeel, Brand, and Segal (1987) suggested that certain personality characteristics might be related to satisfaction in stepfamilies. These include tolerance for ambiguity, cognitive complexity, and personal flexibility.

Training School. The *training school perspective* is that first marriage is a training school for subsequent relationships. The training school perspective has two subhypotheses.

The first subhypothesis postulates positive effects: A person
"graduates" (divorces) from the first marriage with newfound
knowledge regarding the type of person who is right for him or her
and the kinds of behaviors necessary to maintain a successful relationship, knowledge that the person applies to "postgraduate education" (a remarriage) (Dean & Gurak, 1978). Philosopher Sam Keen
(1983) had this perspective in mind when he suggested that people
must first experience what he termed a "neurotic love" (selfish,
self-focused) before they can enjoy an "erotic love" (giving, other-
focused). Although he did not suggest that these two loves had to be
experienced with different partners, for many the erotic love affair is
indeed with someone other than their first partner or spouse.

Support for the positive training school hypothesis is limited.
Albrecht (1979) reported that 88% of postdivorce remarried people said their remarriage was happier than their first marriage had
been, and nearly 66% thought their experiences in the prior marriage aided their remarriage adjustment. In a pair of small-scale
qualitative studies in which Gilligan's theory of moral development was used as a framework, some support was found for the
notion that remarriers had changed as a result of experiences in
their first marriages; remarried women and men reported that
their reasons for remarrying reflected a higher level of care and
responsibility than their reasons for marrying the first time (Byrd
& Smith, 1988; R. Smith, Goslen, Byrd, & Reece, 1991). Unfortunately we cannot determine from these studies whether a causal
link was found between changes in self-reported reasons for marriage and experiences that occurred within the first marriage.
There are a number of competing explanations (e.g., faulty memo-
ries, age-related developmental changes, cognitive dissonance,
social desirability). Other studies have not found support for the
notion that the formerly married profit from their experiences in
ways that contribute either to more satisfying or more stable
remarriages (Dean & Gurak, 1978; Farrell & Markman, 1986).

The second subhypothesis of the training school perspective
suggests that what might be learned in first marriages are negative

patterns of interaction and dysfunctional problem-solving techniques (Brody et al., 1988). These negative marital behaviors learned within the context of first marriages then are transferred into subsequent marriages, making them unsatisfying and unstable. Empirical evidence shows that such negative learning does take place (Furstenberg & Spanier, 1984; Kalmuss & Seltzer, 1986). For example, spousal violence is likely to continue from one marriage to the next (Kalmuss & Seltzer, 1986). Given the short courtship periods and the limited preparation for remarriage, it is perhaps not surprising that people are more likely to transfer learned negative behaviors from the first marriage than they are to learn how to be successfully partnered.

Attitudes Toward Divorce/Willingness to Leave Marriage. This hypothesis proposes that the pool of people who remarry hold *different attitudes* toward divorce as a potential solution to marriage problems than do those in first marriages (Halliday, 1980). Among those in first marriages are some people for whom divorce is not an option. They will stay in empty, unsatisfying marriages because of religious beliefs or for other reasons. The pool of remarried people, however, contains many individuals who already have shown by their behaviors that they consider divorce to be an alternative to an unhappy marriage. This selectivity factor inflates the rate of divorce among remarried couples.

The unwillingness of remarried individuals to stay in an unsatisfying relationship has been labeled "conditional commitment" (Furstenberg & Spanier, 1984). Remarried people (especially those postdivorce) may be fearful of another marital dissolution, but they nonetheless may prefer another divorce to living in a conflictual, unsatisfying relationship. Furstenberg and Spanier (1984) found that remarried people had different, more favorable attitudes toward divorce as a solution to marital problems than they did in their first marriages. Ganong and Coleman (1989) found that nearly a third of their sample of remarried couples had discussed divorce prior to remarriage.

Remarried couples in general, therefore, probably do have different attitudes toward the acceptability of divorce than first-married couples do; whether this finding sufficiently explains the greater divorce rates for remarriages is not clear. Booth and Edwards (1992) found that a willingness to divorce was only weakly related to redivorce.

Dysfunctional Belief Systems. In 20th-century marriages an *ethic of gratification* has replaced an *ethic of obligation* (Bohannon, 1985). The reasons for marrying are increasingly personal ones, having more to do with achieving emotional satisfaction than with survival, duty, and obligation. Marriages, as a result, become more and more important as a source of emotional, psychological, and social fulfillment. Modern Americans believe they have a right to a happy marriage. The definition of what a good spouse is has changed, and the demands placed on marriages have become more abstract and thus harder to meet.

These widespread cultural changes in expectations for marriage have made all marriages more fragile. It has been proposed, however, that the expectations of those who remarry after divorce are unrealistically high and exceed those of the rest of society. Remarriages, therefore, are less stable because a greater percentage of remarriers want more from marriage, and, if their expectations are not met, they dissolve the relationship. They may be more likely than others to pursue an ideal of romantic love and to see romantic love as a necessary component for a good relationship (Goetting, 1982).

Romantic love is portrayed often in our culture as a magical force that cannot be controlled (Hendrick & Hendrick, 1992). One can search for romantic love, but love cannot be forced; it just happens, or one falls into it. Romantic love is described as sexually and emotionally stimulating, mysterious, and all-encompassing (Hendrick & Hendrick, 1992). Unfortunately one also can fall out of romantic love, a process as magical and mysterious as falling in love in the first place. Once partners marry and spend time together, romantic love begins to lessen. If the intense emotional experience of romantic love is how an individual defines love, then when these feelings dissipate, the person will search for a new love relationship (Goetting, 1982).

Unrealistic beliefs and expectations for what should occur in remarried family relationships leads to frustration and disappointment when daily experiences do not match the expectations. Despite the widespread adherence by clinicians to the notions that unrealistic expectations and dysfunctional beliefs about remarriage and stepparenting lead to remarital dissatisfaction and dissolution, little empirical research has been conducted to examine these relations. Kurdek and Fine (1991) found that the strength of belief in stepfamily myths was negatively related to both stepfathers' and mothers' reported adjustment, supporting the hypothesis that belief in stepfamily myths is related to problems. However, the design of this correlational study prevents us from drawing the conclusion that beliefs are causally related to adjustment. In fact, the opposite may be true; poor adjustment could cause individuals to adopt certain beliefs about remarried family life. No research yet has examined the relationship between beliefs and redivorce.

Adherence to myths about divorce and remarriage, irrational beliefs about self and about relationships, and invalid appraisals of life events have been postulated as contributors to marital dissatisfaction in first marriages and remarriages (Baucom & Epstein, 1990; Coleman & Ganong, 1985; Kurdek & Fine, 1991; Visher & Visher, 1988). These cognitive correlates of dissatisfaction likely are related to redivorce as well.

Interpersonal Causes
for Remarital Instability

Social Exchange. Social exchange theory has been used to explain first marriage, divorce, and remarriage. According to this theory, relationships are exchanges between partners; the goods exchanged in relationships include money, love, social support, sex, and various types of assistance, among other things (Giles-Sims, 1987b). Individuals in relationships seek to maximize their benefits while minimizing their losses. For example, Larissa marries Anthony because she perceives that the rewards of being married to Anthony will exceed both the costs of being in the relationship with him (the *comparison level*) and the potential benefits that might be gained by being in a relationship with someone else or remaining single (the *comparison level of alternatives*).

In marriage over time, however, marital rewards often diminish in value, and alternative relationships thus become more attractive. Larissa and Anthony may divorce in order to seek other relationships (remarriages) that will provide them with a better return for their costs. This exchange model, or at least principles from exchange theory, has been used to explain why people remarry and also why some people are more likely to remarry than others (Becker et al., 1977). Positive attributes that divorced people can bargain with include financial incentives (income, education, property), physical attractiveness, social status, and sex. Costs include debts, poor health, and children from a prior relationship. In this model, if costs of divorce are relatively low, some people may look continuously for better partnerships. In other words a marriage contract does not keep them from continuing to shop for relationship bargains. Remarriers also may be more vigilant in assessing the relative distribution of costs and benefits, and they may be more willing to dissolve marriages in order to seek equity. Whether this greater willingness to dissolve marriages is due to previous marital experiences or personal beliefs is unknown.

Contextual Model of Interpersonal Relationships. Based on a model of marital interaction developed by Bradbury and Fincham (1988), this interpersonal perspective hypothesizes that when one spouse behaves, the partner attends to and perceives the behavior, assigns some meaning to it, and then responds with behavior. The period of time between the observable behavior of the spouse and the observable behavior of the partner is called the *processing stage,* in which the behavior of the other is processed cognitively and affectively. An interaction can be seen as comprising many sequences of spouse's behavior → partner's processing → partner's behavior → spouse's processing → spouse's behavior (Bradbury & Fincham, 1990). The processing period is affected by the context in which the interaction sequence occurs. *Context* is a broadly defined concept that includes immediate thoughts and feelings, as well as stable psychological variables that may influence interpretation of a spouse's behaviors (e.g., personality, information processing biases, mood states). This model thus contains individual difference variables, as well as interpersonal variables.

The contextual model is relatively new and has yet to receive much attention from researchers interested in close relationships in stepfamilies. Kurdek (1991a) found some support for this model with remarried couples, however, and it is likely that the contextual model will be examined more frequently in the future.

Societal-Level Causes
for Remarital Instability

Incomplete Institutionalization of Remarriages. We presented (in Chapter 1) some of the assertions of Cherlin's (1978) position that remarried families lack formalized societal support in a variety of ways, including the absence of guidelines and norms to help guide the behaviors of those in remarriages and steprelationships. According to the *incomplete institutionalization hypothesis*, remarriages are less stable than first marriages because of very complex family situations that remarried family members are left to deal with more or less on their own. The combination of new, complicated family dynamics and few guidelines means greater stress on the remarriage, leading to more divorces.

Generally two dimensions of the incomplete institutionalization hypothesis have been examined: the presence of stepchildren and contact with stepkin and quasi-kin. Bohannon (1970) coined the term *quasi-kin* to refer to former spouses, the new partners of former spouses, and the kin of former spouses. These two dimensions are seen as operationalizations of stepfamily complexity and role ambiguity. Contacts with stepkin and quasi-kin usually have been examined as predictors of marital quality in remarriage, and the presence of stepchildren has been examined as a potential predictor of both marital quality and marital stability.

Evidence to support incomplete institutionalization as an explanation for remarriage quality and stability has been mixed. The relation between contact with quasi-kin and marital functioning has received limited support (Clingempeel, 1981; Clingempeel & Brand, 1985). Similarly some researchers have found that children destabilize remarriages and reduce marital quality (Becker et al., 1977; Booth & Edwards, 1992; White & Booth, 1985), and others have found no differences in the divorce rates of remarriages with and without stepchildren (Castro Martin & Bumpass, 1989; Furstenberg & Spanier, 1984). The relation between marital functioning and the presence of children from prior relationships also is unclear; some researchers have found such a relation (Clingempeel, 1981; Clingempeel & Brand, 1985; Koepke, Hare, & Moran, 1992; Pasley & Ihinger-Tallman, 1982), while others have not (Kalmuss & Seltzer, 1986; Schultz, Schultz, & Olson, 1991). Despite the contradictory findings to date, or perhaps because of them, the incomplete institutionalization hypothesis is likely to generate much research in the future.

Socioeconomic Status. Not everyone is equally likely to divorce. Persons of low socioeconomic status more often divorce than persons of high socioeconomic status. Thus the pool of potential remarriers contains a greater proportion of individuals with low incomes, jobs that require little training and provide little employment security, and low levels of education. These persons are under greater economic stress, they have fewer financial and personal resources to withstand threats to their well-being, and it is harder for them to access community support systems. Accordingly the greater incidence of divorce in remarriage is due, at least partially, to the greater risk for divorce of those with low socioeconomic status (Voydanoff, 1990). In fact, Castro Martin and Bumpass (1989) reported that two variables associated with lower socioeconomic attainment—lower educational achievement, and being married the first time as teenagers—statistically accounted for remarriages being less stable than first marriages. This finding lends indirect support for the socioeconomic explanation.

Remarriage Market. With the exception of those who are widowed or divorced at very young ages, most of the people in the remarriage market face a poorer selection of available mates. Within each age cohort the pool of potential eligible partners with similar interests, beliefs, and lifestyles is likely to be relatively small, leading to remarriage between persons who have different backgrounds (Booth & Edwards, 1992). This societal-level explanation suggests that those in the remarriage pool have less control over their mate selection than those in first marriages because they have fewer good choices; that is, if they want to be married, they may have to settle for less desirable "merchandise" because the remarriage market is more limited.

This explanatory model is congruent with some of the other models. For example, the divorce-prone personality hypothesis and the willingness to leave hypothesis are intrapersonal explanations congruent with this societal-level explanation. The remarriage market may contain not only fewer compatible individuals but also an overrepresentation of individuals who are temperamentally or attitudinally poorly suited to being married to anyone.

A Seeming Paradox

The body of literature on remarriage satisfaction, remarriage adjustment, and remarriage quality is relatively large. Most of this research consists of simple comparisons of the marital quality of remarried couples to the marital quality of first-married couples. Cross-sectional studies generally have found little or no difference in the marital quality of remarriages, compared to first marriages (Vemer, Coleman, Ganong, & Cooper, 1989).

If remarriers are as happy as first marriers, why do they divorce more often? Booth and Edwards (1992) suggested that it takes less deterioration in marital quality to precipitate divorce among those who have divorced previously. Therefore cross-sectional designs do not find differences in marital quality between remarriages and first marriages; when marital satisfaction decreases somewhat for remarried couples, they end the marriage. Consequently, although stability is lower for remarriages, marital quality is not, because the couples who remain remarried are those who are still relatively satisfied. Booth and Edwards's explanation has not been tested, although their longitudinal work and the longitudinal studies of others (e.g., Kurdek, 1991b) may yet yield some answers to this seeming paradox. Kurdek (1991b) reported that marital quality decreased over the first year of marriage more rapidly for remarried individuals than for those in first marriages; subsequent assessments of these couples may help shed light on the relation between remarital quality and remarital stability.

Which Explanatory Model Is Best?

Booth and Edwards (1992), in a study that examined five explanatory models, concluded that no single explanation of remarriage stability and quality is sufficient. They found evidence that the incomplete institutionalization hypothesis, the attitudes toward divorce/willingness to leave a marriage hypothesis, the divorce-prone personality hypothesis, and the remarriage market model all contributed to explaining declines in marital quality and redivorce. They cautioned, however, that these findings should not be interpreted too broadly because many couples in remarriages having one or two risk factors obviously find ways to stay happily married (Booth & Edwards, 1992). For example, some couples who enjoy satisfying and stable remarriages live in complex stepfamily systems, perceive divorce as a viable solution to marital unhappiness, and hold high expectations for marriage.

This point deserves further comment. Researchers have made many attempts to document the differences in marital stability and marital quality between first marriages and remarriages. Earlier in this chapter, we presented nine models that have been proposed to explain these differences, and we mentioned several studies designed to assess the validity of these models. We feel compelled to point out, however, that the magnitude of the differences in marital quality and marital stability between remarriages and first marriages (what researchers call *effect sizes*) is generally quite small. To paraphrase Shakespeare, this work may be characterized as "much ado about next to nothing." In fact, some researchers have suggested no need for explanatory models of marital quality differences because, for all practical purposes, the differences are minuscule (Furstenberg & Spanier, 1984).

What may prove to be a more fruitful line of research is the study of processes within remarital relationships. For example, more studies are needed that address such questions as, What factors contribute to satisfaction in remarriages? What do happily remarried couples do that is different from what unhappily remarried couples do? What are the processes by which couples build strong relationships? In the last section of this chapter, we present some of the studies that have focused on remarriage dynamics.

ᴥ Remarriage Dynamics

Building a Couple Bond

Clinicians often identify a strong couple bond as one of the primary requisites for having a successful stepfamily, the rationale being that a strong bond between adult partners is helpful in facilitating the development of positive stepparent-stepchild relationships and serves as a buffer when other family relationships are stressful (Mills, 1984; Visher & Visher, 1988). In family systems theory the task of building a couple bond is conceptualized as establishing a boundary around the marital dyad. The concept of *boundaries* refers to system or subsystem rules that define not only who is in a specific relationship but also what tasks and functions will be performed within that relationship (Minuchin, 1974). Ambiguous or unclear boundaries have been found to be related to increased stress and problems in relationship functioning in nuclear families (Boss & Greenberg, 1984).

In some stepfamilies it may be difficult for couples to establish boundaries around the remarriage relationship in a way that excludes children (Pasley, 1987), particularly if children participated in activities prior to the remarriage that generally are thought to be the purview of the marital dyad (e.g., serving as a parent's confidant, making decisions regarding younger children). When this is the case, it may be difficult to establish the legitimacy of the new partner in the minds of the children. They may see the stepparent as causing them to lose status and power in the family.

Relationships with former partners also can make it difficult to establish boundaries around the remarriage, particularly when former partners are coparenting actively (Roberts & Price, 1989; Weston & Macklin, 1990). Remarried persons who share parenting tasks with former partners have to figure out how to maintain a working relationship as parents, yet not let the former spouse intrude on the remarriage (Crosbie-Burnett, 1989b). This task may be difficult for some individuals because, in nuclear families, parental tasks and marital tasks are usually both fulfilled by the married couple. In remarriages the remarried couple fulfills marital tasks, but parental tasks may continue to be split between the ex-spouses or shared between the ex-spouses (the parents) and the stepparents. As we see in Chapter 4, stepparents do a large share of the child rearing in many stepfamilies, so there is no clear-cut boundary between the marital and parental subsystems in every remarried family.

Unfortunately, few researchers have examined the process of building a couple bond. In a qualitative study of the dialectics of remarriages, Cissna, Cox, and Bochner (1990) found two interactive, simultaneously occurring tasks associated with relationship development in newly formed stepfamilies. The first task was for the remarried couple to establish the solidarity of the marriage in the minds of the stepchildren. The couple did this in two ways: (a) by telling the children that the marriage was the most important relationship to the adults, and (b) by spending time together as a couple, planning how to present a unified front to the children. The second task was to establish parental authority, particularly the credibility of the stepparent. To do this, both the biological parent and the child had to develop trust in the stepparent's ability to act like a parent, to discipline wisely and fairly, and to establish a warm emotional bond with the child.

Power and Equity
in Remarriage Relationships

Several researchers have found that decision making in remarriages tends to be shared fairly equally between partners (e.g., Coleman & Ganong, 1989; Crosbie-Burnett & Giles-Sims, 1991). In fact, evidence shows that remarried women have relatively more power in remarriages, either as a result of men giving up power or because women actively take a greater role in decision making. Hobart (1991) found that remarried men "gave in" to their wives when disagreements arose more often than men in first marriages gave in to their wives; and Coleman and Ganong (1989) reported that women in remarriages purposely sought more control and a larger decision-making role related to financial issues than they had in their first marriages. The remarried women in Furstenberg and Spanier's study (1984) thought the increased responsibilities of being a single parent led them into assuming larger decision-making roles in their remarriages. This shared power is a characteristic that likely holds for homosexual stepfamily couples as well (Koepke et al., 1993), considering that homosexual couples in general, and lesbian couples in particular, value egalitarian relationships (Blumstein & Schwartz, 1983).

Giles-Sims (1987a), using *normative-resource theory*, a corollary of exchange theory, speculated that resources and ideology are factors that help determine post-remarriage marital power relations. Women in remarriages may bring relatively more resources to the marriage, and remarried couples may hold less traditional views about how marital roles should be performed. Ishii-Kuntz and Coltrane (1992) found support for both of these perspectives; remarried wives were more likely than other wives to be employed outside the home, to hold less traditional views, and to earn a greater proportion of the family income. These authors also found less segregation of labor based on gender in remarried families than in first-married families.

Other researchers have not found this same correspondence between decision-making power and involvement in task sharing in remarriages. In a study of remarried fathers and their new wives, Guisinger, Cowan, and Schuldberg (1989) found that couples described their decision making as egalitarian, but their division of household labor tended to be split along traditional gender lines. This finding means that the women in this sample were doing the vast majority of the household work, including most of the child care for their stepchildren. Demo and Acock (1993), in a nationally drawn sample, found that couples in stepfather households also adhered to a traditional, gender-based division of household tasks. Mothers in remarried families did not differ from mothers in first marriages in the amount of household work they did, and both groups of women did far more than their husbands. Despite the discrepancy in the amount of domestic work being done by husbands and wives, remarried mothers described the division of household tasks as generally fair to both partners.

In contrast, many of the stepmothers in the Guisinger et al. (1989) study did not think the amount of work their husbands did was enough. Their dissatisfaction grew over the first 3 years of remarriage, and they were particularly displeased with the division of labor related to child care. Marital satisfaction of both husbands and wives was related to how satisfied they were with the degree to which child care, household tasks, and decision making were shared. Marital satisfaction also was related to the *perception* that household chores, child care, and decision making were divided equitably.

These research findings that task sharing is related to remarital happiness are congruent with clinical assertions that remarried families fare better when the adults do not adhere to sex role stereotypes to guide their beliefs and behaviors (Carter, 1988). Exploring the links between decision making, equity, and the distribution of power in remarriage holds considerable potential for future research on close relationships.

Communication and Conflict Management
in Remarriages

It is commonly believed that remarried couples fight with each other more than couples in first marriages. This belief is not surprising. After all, in addition to the normal stressors that confront every couple that has children, remarried couples must deal also with unique stressors associated with stepfamily living. The primary topics that remarried couples argue about are issues related to children from prior relationships (e.g., rules for children's behavior, discipline techniques) and financial issues (Hobart, 1991; Messinger, 1976).

Remarried couples have been found to possess poorer conflict resolution and problem-solving skills and to be more coercive toward each other than couples in first marriages (Bray, Berger, Silverblatt, & Hollier, 1987; Larson & Allgood, 1987). Remarried couples also agree less often about marital issues and are less accurate in their perceptions of each other's values and beliefs about marital issues than first-marriage couples (Farrell & Markman, 1986). Farrell and Markman speculated that remarried couples were less skillful communicators because of low self-esteem, fear of conflict, and because they chose partners who would fulfill their immediate needs (financial needs for women, reduced loneliness for men) without regard for how well these partners could communicate with them and relate to them intimately.

Not all researchers have found remarried couples to be deficient communicators compared to first-marriage couples, however. Anderson and White (1986) found that functional stepfamilies were more able to reach agreement than dysfunctional stepfamilies, functional nuclear families, and dysfunctional nuclear families. In another study remarried couples in therapy for a child-focused problem and remarried couples not in therapy reported better communication and problem-solving skills than the normative sample on ENRICH, a measure of marital dynamics (Brown, Green, & Druckman, 1990). The authors of this study speculated that remarried couple relationships tend to be strong and functional even in stepfamilies that are having some problems. These findings, and the researchers' speculations, are somewhat surprising.

Other findings on remarital communication also are unexpected, if not surprising. Some researchers have found that communication and conflict resolution skills are not related to marital satisfaction for remarried couples (Farrell & Markman, 1986; Larson & Allgood, 1987). This finding is inconsistent with what would be hypothesized, in light of the presumed importance of clear communication in creating satisfying marital relationships, and it differs from the relation found between communication skills and marital satisfaction in first marriages (Farrell & Markman, 1986; Larson & Allgood, 1987). The findings suggest that remarriage satisfaction may have less to do with affective exchanges between partners than does first-marriage satisfaction. Farrell and Markman conjectured that remarriers may be more interested in the direct, instrumental rewards they receive from marriage (e.g., tangible things the spouse does for them), rather than indirect, expressive rewards (e.g., feeling loved and valued by the spouse). This speculation is consistent with the more pragmatic reasons given for remarriage, but it has not yet been empirically tested. Obviously much is yet to be learned about communication in remarried families.

A number of moderating and mediating variables potentially influence the dynamics of remarriages. Among them are ages of partners; children (e.g., where they live, how many, how old, gender, legal custody); frequency of contact and nature of relationships with former spouses; contact and support from extended kin; marital expectations; belief systems and ideologies (about marriage, parenting); socioeconomic status; education; prior marital histories of both partners; partner personalities, both individually and collectively; and interpersonal skills brought by each partner into the relationship. This lengthy list is nonetheless a partial one; many other variables likely affect the functioning of remarriages. Unfortunately this list also represents a considerable amount of conjecture; some of these variables have rarely or never been studied.

Clearly much more examination of remarriage relationships is needed. The existing literature on remarriages illustrates some of the problems we mention in Chapter 1; for example, remarried family complexity is often not adequately addressed, and too many researchers spend too much time and energy looking for and explaining small differences between first marriages and remarriages, often ignoring similarities. The literature on remarriage is noteworthy for two reasons, however. First, research on the remarried couple has been guided by theory to a greater extent than research on other remarried family relationships. Second, a relatively large number of remarriage researchers have taken a developmental view, looking at changes in remarriage dynamics over time or examining the effects of antecedent events/conditions/variables on subsequent remarriage dynamics.

4

Stepparent-Stepchild
Relationships

The stepparent-stepchild relationship is perhaps the most heavily scrutinized close relationship within remarried families. It is believed by many to be the most important relationship in predicting overall stepfamily happiness (Crosbie-Burnett, 1984; Visher & Visher, 1988), and it generally is considered to be the most problematic and stressful relationship (Mills, 1984). In fact, the presence of stepchildren within remarried households is a destabilizing influence and a major contributor to the somewhat greater rate of divorce among couples with stepchildren relative to those without stepchildren (Booth & Edwards, 1992; McCarthy, 1978; Teachman, 1986; White & Booth, 1985).

✒ Residential and Nonresidential Stepparents

Researchers have not always been clear about which stepparents and which stepchildren they are studying when examining stepparent-stepchild relationships. For example, researchers are often vague about whether only residential stepparents are being studied or whether residential and nonresidential stepparents are combined in the same sample. It is also often not clear whether only residential stepchildren are studied or whether nonresidential ones are mixed in as well. Worse yet, in some samples stepchildren and children born to the remarried couple are not differentiated. The importance of defining the specific relationship and distinguishing between family and household when providing stepfamily sample description is critical if the data on close relationships are to be interpreted in a meaningful way.

The following examples provide an idea of the problems associated with examining close relationships between stepparent and stepchild:

1. Lena recently married Derrick. Derrick has had no contact with his two school-aged children since he divorced their mother more than 8 years ago. Although Lena would be considered a stepmother to Derrick's two children, she has had no contact with them whatsoever. There is no relationship. This is not a unique situation; many fathers lose contact with their children after divorce (Furstenberg & Nord, 1985).

2. Sarah recently married Joel, whose two school-aged children visit every other weekend and during the summer. In this case we would define Sarah as a *nonresidential* stepmother, meaning that she is a stepmother to stepchildren who do not reside with her most of the time. From Sarah's perspective, the affective relationship she has with Joel's children may range from very close to very distant, and it is quite possible that she may feel differently about each child, emotionally close to one and more distant from the other. Each child also might feel differently about his or her relationship with Sarah. One child might feel very close, and another child might feel distant. The congruency among the rat-

ings of stepparent and stepchild would not necessarily be high; sometimes stepparents may feel close to a child who does not feel close to them, and vice versa.

3. Maria recently married José. He has joint physical custody of his two school-aged children. They spend half the week with Maria and José, and half the week with their mother. Maria is a stepmother, but there is no unambiguous adjective for the type of stepmother she is. Is she a semiresidential stepmother, a part-time residential stepmother, or should some new term be applied in this case? The quality and closeness of step-relationships could range similarly to those described in Example 2.

4. LaDonna recently married George. George has sole legal custody of his children; they live with him most of the time and visit their mother occasionally. LaDonna, in this case, is a *residential* stepmother. Once again, the closeness of relationships could range from very close to very distant with one or both children.

5. Fiona recently married Tom. Tom has full custody of his son, who lives with him most of the time and visits his mother occasionally. His daughter lives with Tom's ex-wife and visits Tom and Fiona occasionally. Fiona is a *residential* stepmother to the son and a *nonresidential* stepmother to the daughter. Once again, relationships could range from very close to very distant with one or both children.

Other stepmother combinations are possible, and there is a comparable stepfather relationship for each stepmother combination. *Complex stepfamilies,* those in which both adults are stepparents, provide even more possible permutations. For example, couples may have mutual children plus biological children from previous marriages all living together in the same household, or some children may live in the household and some may live with the other parent.

Where a stepchild lives is not a trivial matter in making sense of the stepparent-stepchild relationship. Sharing a residence creates more opportunities to interact and to develop a close relationship than is the case if stepparents and stepchildren spend time together on a few days or weeks per year. Expectations for role enactment differ, depending on whether stepparents are in contact with the stepchild daily, rarely, or never. The impact of stepparent-stepchild relationships on other close relationships in the stepfamily also is likely to be dependent on the amount of contact between the various relationship members.

The residence of a stepchild is also important to know because residence generally is related to the gender of the stepparent. After divorce, 90% of children of divorced parents live with their mothers (Weitzman, 1988). Consequently most stepmothers are nonresidential stepparents; they acquire nonresidential stepchildren when they marry men who are noncustodial fathers. For the same reason, most stepfathers live in the same household as their stepchildren. Gender is an important variable in understanding stepparents' relationships with stepchildren because a number of relationship dynamics are related to gender expectations and gender role behaviors. Gender issues are discussed more fully later in this chapter.

❧ Models for Stepparenting

Whether stepparents are residential or nonresidential, they have a difficult position in the remarried family. Because the parent-child bond predates the remarriage, the stepparent begins the remarriage as an "outsider." Papernow's (1993) developmental model, which we discuss more fully in Chapter 6, is especially useful in explaining the dynamics of the beginning stages of the stepfamily, particularly the stepfamily household. The *fantasy stage,* a beginning stage of remarriage, finds the biological parent hoping his or her new spouse will be a better partner and also a better parent than the previous spouse. The stepparent hopes to meet these expectations and be appreciated for his or her efforts. For example, if the mother remarried because she felt that she needed parenting assistance with the children, the stepfather is likely to begin trying immediately to be a parent to his stepchildren. This behavior may create problems with everyone: The child resents someone who has yet to develop a strong bond with him or her telling the child what to do, the mother may not approve of the way the stepfather disciplines, and the stepfather may feel angry because he did what was expected and no one appreciated it!

The old television series *The Brady Bunch* is an ill-chosen family model for many remarried couples in the fantasy stage. Unlike this popular television sitcom, strong family ties and warm stepparent-stepchild relationships do not develop instantly.

The reality of typical stepfamily dynamics sets in during the *immersion stage* (Papernow, 1993). It is especially during this stage that the stepparent feels like an outsider. Feelings of jealousy, resentment, confusion, and inadequacy may surface as the closeness of the biological parent-child relationship becomes more obvious to the stepparent. It may also become clear during this stage that the stepparent and parent view the children quite differently. In general, stepparents tend to believe the parent is too lenient with the children; the parent, in turn, believes the stepparent is too harsh and does not understand the children well. These differing viewpoints about the children can become major family stressors (Furstenberg, 1987; Ganong & Coleman, in press; Thomson, McLanahan, & Curtin, 1992).

In another developmental model, Bohannon (1984) uses Galinsky's (1981) stages of parenting as a model for explaining the vicissitudes of stepparenting. The first stage of parenting is the *image-making stage*. In the nuclear family this stage coincides with pregnancy. In the stepfamily, Bohannon believes this stage occurs during the courtship of the child's biological parent and the potential stepparent. It is during this stage that the biological parent and the stepparent begin to think about what sort of parents or stepparents they will be and how these roles will affect their relationship with each other. They also may fantasize about what the child will be like in this new family. If the stepparent and stepchild have spent considerable time together, the stepparent may have a reasonably accurate image of what to expect. The nonresidential stepparent likely will have spent less time with the stepchild, and thus the image may be less realistic.

Galinsky describes the *nurturing stage,* the second stage of parenting, as the time from birth until the child learns to say no. Developing strong attachment is the major parenting task, along with reconciling the real infant with the imaged child. This nurturing stage is difficult for stepparents. First, the stepchild may be anywhere from a few weeks old to an adult when the remarriage occurs. Older stepchildren, particularly adolescents and young adults, may not be receptive to a nurturing stepparent. Clinicians have pointed out that a warm, nurturant stepparent sometimes arouses resistance in stepchildren, who fear being disloyal to their deceased/nonresidential biological parent if they warm up to the stepparent.

Some stepparents, particularly stepfathers, skip the nurturing stage entirely. They see their primary stepparenting task as disciplining the stepchild, and they may be unaware of the need to develop a bond of attachment before attempting to discipline children. In raising children, biological parents often use the attachment they have with their children as part of their discipline technique. For example, when a mother tells her children she is disappointed in them when they have misbehaved, this communication works as a deterrent to future misbehavior because the children care about their mother's approval. The children care because they have an emotional bond with their mother. Stepparents who skip the nurturing stage may find themselves being ineffective at administering the very same discipline strategies that are effective with their own biological children, with whom they have a bond (Mills, 1984).

Some stepparents who want to nurture their stepchildren nonetheless may have a hard time doing so because they lack experience interacting with children. Childless stepparents may attempt, inappropriately, to bond with stepchildren by engaging the children in age-inappropriate activities or by expecting more emotional responsiveness from children than is developmentally normal. However, it may not greatly matter what attempts a stepparent makes to bond with a child. According to Brown et al. (1990), the parent role behavior initiated by the stepparent is less important to stepfamily functioning than is the receptivity of the stepchild to that behavior. If the stepchild is not receptive, there is little the stepparent can do to improve the situation.

Although there is social pressure for stepparents to form attachment bonds with stepchildren fairly rapidly, these expectations actually may work against the stepparent who is trying to be nurturant. Visher and Visher (1988) referred to this pressure as the "myth of instant love." If love does not develop instantly because the stepparent cannot force those warm feelings, he or she feels guilty. If nurturing is resisted by the child, the stepparent may feel defeated and withdraw from further attempts to bond (Hetherington & Clingempeel, 1992). Incidentally Mills (1984) proposed that it takes as many years for the stepparent and stepchild to become attached to each other as the age the child is when the stepparent begins relating to him or her. Although Mills's proposal is a clinical impression that has not been empirically examined, it is a provocative assertion that raises questions about how long Galinsky's nurturing stage might last in stepfamilies.

The third parenting stage begins when the child learns to say no and is referred to by Galinsky (1981) as the *authority stage*. Good parents need to know their child well and adapt to the changes that growth and development bring about. It is at this stage that parents begin to assign motives to the child's behavior, and the child's self-esteem may be greatly influenced by the definition the parents give to the child's behavior. This is an extremely difficult stage in the stepfamily. Establishing the authority of the stepparent is an ongoing task of all the stages and is often a painful process. It is probably typical for stepparents and parents to assign differing motives to children's behaviors. After all, a parent has known the child much longer than the stepparent, and the parent may have a kind of built-in biological bias toward his or her own flesh and blood. Coleman and Ganong (1986b) found that a nearly universal phenomenon among the 100 couples they interviewed was the different definitions the parents and stepparents attributed to the behaviors of the same child. These varied attributions about children's motives for behaving led to attributions regarding the adult partner: On the one hand, the biological parent inevitably thought the stepparent's view of the child's behavior was unreasonably negative and the expectations too high; the stepparent, on the other hand, believed the biological parent was blindly optimistic and too reluctant to establish authority.

The *interpretative stage* of parenting is roughly the same as the *latency period*, the period when children are of school age. The parent's major task is to explain the cultural and physical world to the child. Parents also begin to interpret themselves to the child at this stage. In turn, the child begins to develop an image defining good and bad parenting. In the stepfamily the child is likely to check everything the stepparent says about the world with one of his or her biological parents. If the nonresidential parent disagrees with the stepparent's view of the world, the stepchild is likely to discard the stepparent's view as inaccurate. When the stepchild consistently rejects the stepparent's worldview, a close relationship is unlikely to develop. The relationship may become strained and distant. Adolescent and adult stepchildren may actively reject having the world interpreted to them. If stepchildren are uninterested in the stepparent's values and beliefs about how things are, the stepparent may withdraw or become hostile toward the child.

Galinsky defined the *interdependent stage* of parenting as beginning shortly before the child's puberty. This stage is typically difficult for all parents but may be especially problematic in stepfamilies. Children are beginning to pull away from and challenge their parents, and Galinsky said it is important that parents not misinterpret this behavior. Children at this age want to be treated as adults even though their behavior is often not very mature. In stepfamilies the adult family members may be trying to make the family unit become more cohesive, to feel more like their image of how a family should feel. Stepchildren may resent being pulled back into the family, not necessarily because of objections to the stepparent or to the new stepfamily, but because it seems like a return to a more dependent status when they are seeking adulthood.

The final stage identified by Galinsky is *departure*. She stated that biological parents often mistakenly imagine that their relationship with their partners will return to what it was before the children were born. Stepparents make a similar mistake of imagining that with the stepchildren out of the home, they can begin making the marital relationship what they had always wanted it to be. There is little if any evidence that either of these images is realistic.

As difficult as it may be for biological parents to deal with the tasks Galinsky (1981) defined, it is much harder for stepparents. Bohannon (1984) speculated that many of the stages Galinsky defined are phase-inappropriate in stepfamilies; that is, the stepfamily is out of sync, compared to nuclear families. In fact, stepparents may feel as if they must master multiple tasks at once, trying to both develop an attachment to and discipline a child who may be trying actively to become independent of adults in the family. It is difficult to successfully adapt nuclear family models of parenting to stepfamily dynamics. In Chapter 6 models designed especially for stepfamilies are discussed.

❧ Stepmother-Stepchild Relationships

Nearly everyone is exposed first to stepmother-stepchild relationships through fairy tales such as "Cinderella," "Hansel and Gretel," and "Snow White." These ancient stories (the story of Cinderella has been traced back to ninth-century China) focusing on the wicked, uncaring stepmother have contributed to one of the best known cross-cultural stereotypes (Noy, 1991; Wald, 1981). Unfortunately this well-known stereotype may interfere with appropriate socialization for a common family position; that is, although a large percentage of American women "grow up" to be stepmothers, socialization for this role is not a part of the culture. Little girls may play with dolls of differing ethnic and racial background, dolls that come complete with adoption papers, and dolls of differing genders, but they do not play with stepchild dolls. And although little girls commonly say, "When I grow up I want to be a mommy," we have never heard of a child saying, "I want to be a stepmommy when I grow up." With a long history of negative fairy tale images and little or no socialization for the stepmother role, it is no wonder the stepmother-stepchild relationship is viewed often with some trepidation by both stepmothers and stepchildren.

Despite the cultural beliefs that stepmothers are mean and "wicked," there have been few investigations of the behaviors of stepmothers. Some empirical evidence supports the cultural stereotypes, however. For example, investigators have found that stepmothers have more problematic relationships with stepchildren than do stepfathers, and stepmother families are the most likely of all stepfamily types to have conflict and poor adjustment (Clingempeel

& Segal, 1986; Hobart, 1987, 1989; Kurdek & Fine, 1993; Zill, 1988). It also has been found that stepmothers are less satisfied with their relationships with stepchildren than are stepfathers (Ahrons & Wallisch, 1987; Hobart, 1987) and that stepmothers display more negative behaviors toward stepchildren than do stepfathers (Hetherington, 1987; Santrock & Sitterle, 1987). These negative behaviors do not extend to child abuse, however, which is more common in stepfather families (Giles-Sims & Finkelhor, 1984).

Stepmother families appear to be especially stressed when visits between the stepchild and the nonresidential biological mother are frequent (Clingempeel & Segal, 1986; Furstenberg & Nord, 1985), and nonresidential mothers tend to remain in contact with their children, certainly more so than nonresidential fathers (Furstenberg & Nord, 1985; Seltzer & Bianchi, 1988). It has been suggested that mothers' frequent contact may interfere with the development of a strong bond between stepmothers and children, resulting in more stress and conflict in the stepmother household (Clingempeel & Segal, 1986). A majority of stepmothers in a study by Brown (1987) acknowledged that the most troublesome stepfamily relationship at first was their relationship with the stepchildren's biological mother. It was also difficult for the stepmothers to accept the close relationship between their stepchildren and the children's biological mother. It is believed that because children's attachment to mothers is greater than their attachment to fathers, children experience more loyalty conflicts and have more trouble adding "another mother" to the family than they do adding another father (Hobart, 1987). These loyalty conflicts may heighten the tension in the stepmother family household.

Considering the overwhelming tendency of the courts to grant physical custody to biological mothers, it is likely that residential stepmother households formed after divorce have unique dynamics that contribute to conflict. Until recently, fathers were awarded custody of their children only when the mother was seen as "unfit" in some way (e.g., a substance abuser). More recently, intense power struggles between the divorcing partners have sometimes resulted in physical custody of the children being awarded to the father. The power struggles between these fiery foes (Ahrons & Rodgers, 1987) usually carry over into the remarried family, putting the stepmother in a very vulnerable position.

Other reasons suggested for the more problematic stepmother-stepchild dynamics are attributed to the socialization of women. Although Thomson et al. (1992) found evidence to suggest that parental roles are less gendered in stepmother families than in stepfather families or original two-parent families, other researchers have found that women's roles within the stepfamily household tend to be quite traditional (Morrison & Thompson-Guppy, 1985). Thus once the stepmother takes on the role of wife to her new husband, she quickly is expected to begin rearing her husband's children as well. In fact, a group of 22 Canadian stepmothers seeking help at two different mental health clinics reported feeling as though they had to prove they were not wicked stepmothers. As a result they overcompensated by providing total care for the stepchildren in the traditionally expected female role. In some cases they provided care to the extent that both biological parents opted out from child care (Morrison & Thompson-Guppy, 1985).

The majority of these Canadian stepmothers indicated they were embarrassed that they had to ask for help. For several of them the stepmother role was the first situation they had encountered that they felt unable to master. Well over half of the stepmothers expressed anger and resentment toward their husbands because they did not set limits for the children, did not support the stepmothers in their parenting role, and often excluded them from the father-child relationship. They were afraid to express this anger to the husband, however, for fear of losing his affection. Additionally, at least 18 of the 22 women expressed identity confusion regarding the stepmother role, feelings of helplessness and ineffectiveness in the home, and feelings of exhaustion or burnout (Morrison & Thompson-Guppy, 1985).

In contrast, other researchers have found some evidence that stepmothers are more satisfied when they carry out traditional roles within the family. For example, Skyles (1983), as reported in Crosbie-Burnett (1988), found that stepmothers who reported high participation in parenting also reported better marital adjustment than stepmothers with low participation in parenting. Nevertheless, immediately taking on parenting behaviors, such as discipline, without an extended period of mutual bonding places the stepmother-stepchild relationship at risk. This is especially true

in those stepfamilies where jealousy and competition exist between the stepmother and the biological mother.

Yet another reason why stepmother households may be more
problematic is there are so few of them. There are fewer stepmother role models to offset the negative images. Stepmothers
may not know any other women who are in similar family situations, so they may think there are few people in whom to confide
or from whom to ask advice. In Western culture women are expected to be in charge of the emotional needs of family members,
and responsibility for the functioning of the family disproportion-
ately falls on women. Consequently, stepmothers who are struggling with their roles, or stepmothers who have ambivalent feelings
about their stepchildren, may be reluctant to ask questions of
anyone not in a stepfamily, for fear of being seen as a failure at one
of women's chief tasks. It is not unlikely that some well-meaning
stepmothers struggle in isolation to do the best they can, rather
than to seek professional advice or other assistance. They may be
embarrassed by their feelings of ineptness and reluctant to be seen
as the wicked "stepmonster" (Morrison & Thompson-Guppy, 1985).

Stepchildren may face similar difficult situations. Ihinger-Tallman (1988) speculated that because there are fewer residential
stepmothers, there will be fewer conversations between children
and their peers about stepmothers. Young children may find that
their friends know the stereotype of the wicked stepmother but
very little else about stepmothers. Both stepchildren and their
stepmothers may feel isolated and unique.

Nonresidential Stepmother-Stepchild Relations

Even though residential stepmothers represent a very small minority of the stepfamily population, we know more about them than
we know about the more numerous nonresidential stepmothers. One
thing we do know about nonresidential stepmothers is that they feel
more ambivalent about their stepchildren than residential stepmothers, although both groups feel some ambivalence. In fact, Ambert
(1986) found that 54% of the stepmothers whose stepchildren lived
with their biological mothers indicated they thought their marriage
would be happier without the stepchildren. Only 30% of stepmoth-

ers who had stepchildren living with them thought this way. And 53% of the nonresidential stepmothers in one of our studies indicated they either dreaded or had ambivalent feelings about the stepchildren's visits (Weddle, 1993). For 25% of the nonresidential stepmothers, the most difficult part about the visiting relationships was having an undefined role with their stepchildren.

Not surprisingly, nonresidential stepmothers also report more stress than residential stepmothers (Ambert, 1986). Ihinger-Tallman (1988) speculated that this difference may be due to the standard of comparison available to stepmothers who have stepchildren going in and out of the home; they know what life is like with and without the stepchildren and many prefer life without them. Stepmothers whose stepchildren live with them do not have this comparative framework, although Ihinger-Tallman posited that residential stepmothers may be more positive because being with stepchildren on a daily basis provides more opportunities to build a close relationship.

We also speculate that the proximity in ages sometimes found between nonresidential stepmothers and their stepchildren may create relationships resembling the dynamics of siblings more than those of parents and children. Howe (1986) reported that the greater the maternal involvement in play or attention given to either of two siblings, the less friendly the interaction between the siblings. Perhaps the greater the attention the father pays to either his child or his wife (the nonresidential stepmother), the less friendly the interaction will be between his child and his wife. This theoretical explanation may account for some of the jealousy and ill-will between nonresidential stepmothers and visiting stepchildren.

Changes in Stepmother-Stepchild Relationships Over Time. Not much is known about how relationships between stepmothers and stepchildren change over time. Some researchers found that stepmother-stepdaughter relationships became more positive (Clingempeel & Segal, 1986); others found that women became less optimistic about stepmothering over time and also developed less positive attitudes toward their stepchildren (Guisinger et al., 1989). Theoretically, so many variables could contribute to changes in stepmother-stepchild relationships over time that it is difficult to speculate in what directions the relationships might change or what factors might influence those changes. For instance, demographic characteristics such as the number of stepchildren, the number of the stepmother's biological children, age of the stepchildren, gender of the stepchildren, and frequency of contact between stepmother and stepchildren may all be factors in relationship changes. Intrapersonal characteristics such as values, beliefs, cognitive styles, temperaments, and personality traits may be factors, as may changes in other individuals and relationships. Virtually none of these variables have been studied to assess changes in stepmother-stepchild relationships.

One researcher has speculated, however, about the potential influences of the father on relationships between stepmothers and stepchildren in complex stepfamilies. Hobart (1988) suggested that a father may contribute to the relationship problems between his wife and his children if he is more lenient or generous with his nonresidential children than he is with his wife's children (his stepchildren) who live in the home. His wife may resent his behavior and come to dislike his children as well because they are part of the source of her stress. Her resentment, in turn, may be picked up by the stepchildren, who react with hostility or anxiety that further erodes the stepmother-stepchild relationship. Hobart reported that as a result of the difficulties between stepmother and stepchild, the father-child relationship may deteriorate as well.

A number of factors appear to contribute to the perception that the stepmother-stepchild relationship is one of the most difficult family relationships to develop and positively maintain. Many of these factors are due to the ambiguously defined role of the stepmother. However, the stepchild is not an inert player in this family drama. Some stepchildren purposively may resist forming a close relationship with their stepmother out of loyalty to their biological mother. In such cases, no matter what the stepmother does to attempt to build a close relationship, she probably is doomed to failure, at least in the short run.

❧ Stepfather-Stepchild Relationships

Until recently stepfathers have avoided many of the negative cultural stereotypes attributed to stepmothers. Researchers, however, have not ignored stepfathers. In fact, much of the stepfamily research that burgeoned during the last decade was on stepfather households (Coleman & Ganong, 1990). This growth was partly because stepfather households greatly outnumber other types of stepfamily households: 82% of all stepfamily households are stepfather households (Glick, 1989). Because they are more numerous, stepfather households are easier for researchers to locate. Therefore researchers often have limited their samples to the more accessible stepfather-stepchildren relationships.

Stepfathers Who Also Are Fathers. The dynamics of stepfather-stepchild relationships seem to differ, depending on whether the stepfather is also a biological father or not. Stepfathers who have biological children of their own seem to fare better in stepfamily households. They feel more companionship with their stepchildren, experience more intimate stepfather-stepchild interactions, are more involved with their stepchildren's friends, feel fewer negative feelings about stepchildren, and have fewer desires to escape. This finding is especially true when the oldest stepchild is relatively young (Palisi, Orleans, Caddell, & Korn, 1991).

Biological children may serve to enhance stepfather-stepchild relations in several ways. If the biological children and stepchildren are of similar ages, they may become playmates, establish friendly relations, and provide companionship, emotional support, and affection for each other. Stepfathers may be drawn closer to their stepchildren, and they may have fewer negative attitudes toward them because of the strategies they adopt in striving to treat both sets of children in an equitable manner. The presence of their biological children in the household, in effect, may force men to parent to a greater extent than if they merely had been absorbed into a preexisting family. Finally, it is possible that fathers who have joint or sole custody of their own biological children are selectively those who are more committed to the parental role. It can be argued that these men might be psychologically predisposed toward a positive perception of the parental role and a greater commitment to parenting (Palisi et al., 1991).

Perhaps men with children from a previous relationship fare better in stepfamilies because they are often less inclined to take on a strong parenting role, especially early in the remarriage. They may have less need to play that role with their stepchildren, although other motives have been suggested as well. Crosbie-Burnett (1989b) found less competition between the men in complex stepfamilies (the father and stepfather) and concluded that stepfathers who are participating actively in raising their own biological children are either not attempting to function in the father role with their stepchildren or can cofather better. Because both men in these complex stepfamily situations frequently are also nonresidential fathers, they may have more empathy for each other.

Stepfathers without children of their own probably have had limited experiences being around children and helping to care for them. Men in our culture are not expected to be as active as women in caring for children. As a result, young males spend very little time learning child care roles, and they are provided with fewer opportunities to practice relating to children. Stepfathers who have not parented before simply may lack some of the skills necessary for raising children. Stepfathers who also are fathers may have more realistic expectations for children. They also may invest less emotionally in their stepchildren than stepfathers who are not also biological fathers. Although this situation may sound cold, perhaps it facilitates the gradual development of a mutually satisfying stepfather-stepchild relationship better than when the stepfather tries too hard, too soon (Papernow, 1993; Visher & Visher, 1988).

Whether stepfathers are fathers or not, they may have problems assuming the stepfather identity (Fast & Cain, 1966). Stepparents of both genders, studied by Whitsett and Land (1992), reported that they were not sure what would be involved in being a stepparent and that they also were not sure of their spouse's expectations for them in the stepparenting role. This problem may be especially acute for stepfathers because the paternal role, in general, is less well defined than the maternal role, causing fathers to look to their wives for parenting clues (Tinsley & Parke, 1987). When this phenomenon occurs in the early stages of stepfamily formation, the wife is apt to push the stepfather to function as if he were the biological father of his stepchildren (Papernow, 1993).

Men who are already fathers may be less willing to let their wives define their relationship with the stepchildren than are men who have no experience at fathering. This possibility also may explain why men without children of their own are more likely to compete with the biological father. Stepfathers who follow their wife's lead may try to take an early and active role in disciplining the children, a practice that has been found to impede, rather than enhance, stepfamily integration (Hetherington, Cox, & Cox, 1985; Visher & Visher, 1982). Perhaps stepfathers with no prior parenting experience could benefit from imitating the role models provided by stepfathers who function as nurturing men in children's lives, complementing the biological father's role but not competing with it.

Changes in Stepfather-Stepchild Relationships Over Time. As with stepmother-stepchild relationships, little research addresses changes in stepfathers' relationships with their stepchildren over time. A small body of research on stepfather-stepchild relationships is developing, however, that provides support for Papernow's (1993) model of early stepfamily development. During early development, unrealistically high expectations regarding stepfather-stepchild relationships are followed by a phase of dealing with the realities of stepparenting. Hetherington and Clingempeel (1992) found that after initial attempts to form a positive relationship with the stepchild and to enhance integration of the new family unit, many stepfathers became increasingly disengaged from their stepchildren. Interestingly it was the stepchildren in this study who appeared to shape the stepfathers' behavior. A stepfather would make overtures to the child early in the remarriage, attempt to share information, and engage in other rapport-building activities, only to be ignored. After several attempts at becoming closer, the stepfather responded to being ignored by withdrawing from the child. Considering these findings, it is not surprising that the stepfather-stepchild relationship often becomes more negative and less positive over time (Bray, 1992).

Being ignored by stepchildren is extremely uncomfortable for some men we call "heroes." These men may have married primarily to "save" their new wives and stepchildren. They might be likened to a Clint Eastwood character in a western: Their fantasy is that they will ride into Dodge City, clean up the problems, and make the town safe again, thereby garnering the undying gratitude and respect of the townspeople. If the efforts of a hero stepfather to clean up the problems are not appreciated by his new wife and stepchildren, he may feel that he has failed in his rescue efforts. Failure threatens his self-image, and he withdraws as a defense mechanism.

≈ Child Abuse in Stepfamilies

Perhaps because of the many fairy tales portraying the stepchild as abused and unwanted, considerable attention has been given to the incidence of child abuse in stepfamilies. Although it is widely believed that stepchildren are at risk for child abuse, the findings from empirical studies are mixed.

A number of investigators have painted a very bleak picture of child abuse in stepfamilies, beginning with the landmark survey conducted by Gil (1970), who found that stepfathers or father substitutes were responsible for one-third of reported cases of child abuse. Finkelhor (1987) found that incest was four to five times more common in stepfamilies and that stepdaughters were also more likely to be abused by other men, especially friends of their stepfather. Russell (1984) determined from a random sample of women in San Francisco that one out of every six who had a stepfather as a principal figure in her childhood years was abused sexually by him. It should be noted that the data were from self-reports, the abuse had not necessarily been officially reported, and that Russell defined sexual abuse quite broadly, ranging from unwanted but nonforceful kissing to forcible rape.

More recently, Margolin (1992) found mothers' boyfriends (who might be considered de facto stepfathers) were overrepresented in reported child abuse in Iowa. Father substitutes (e.g., boyfriends) in Britain also showed higher rates of overall sexual abuse of prepubescent girls than biological fathers and stepfathers. Although stepfathers were more likely than fathers to abuse stepchildren, they were less likely to subject them to intercourse (Gordon &

Creighton, 1988). In this study 37% of those abused by biological fathers were forced to have intercourse, compared with 21% of the victims of father substitutes (e.g., boyfriends) and only 16% of the victims of stepfathers. When using the same categories of sexual severity as Russell (1984), Gordon and Creighton (1988) found no differences between the biological fathers, stepfathers, and father substitutes. Malkin and Lamb (1989), as reported in Gelles and Harrop (1991), also concluded from 1984 data on child abuse reports submitted to the American Humane Association that step-parents were at no greater risk of physically abusing children than biological parents. Finally, Gelles and Harrop (1991), using data from the Second National Family Violence Survey, found the rate of overall violence was significantly lower for stepchildren than all other children; sexual abuse was not examined.

Drawing conclusions from the empirical work on child abuse in stepfamilies is difficult. It is not always clear whether the stepfather category includes legal stepfathers only or if de facto stepfathers (mothers' boyfriends) are included as well. Sometimes other male figures such as uncles, grandfathers, and siblings are included with stepfathers, and sometimes they are in a loosely defined "other" category. To add to the confusion, researchers define child abuse in various ways. For example, some studies of child abuse include sexual abuse as one category, other studies include only sexual abuse, and still others completely omit sexual abuse as a category. Samples vary considerably as well. Data are only from officially reported cases of abuse in some instances, from random telephone surveys or clinicians' reports in other instances, and some reports combine officially reported abuse cases with other data. Because of the sensitive nature of the information, nearly all child abuse data are somewhat suspect. Victims and other family members may be more reluctant to report sexual abuse by a biological father than by a stepfather or other male. This is especially likely when the family is financially dependent on the father. Because of cultural stereotypes related to abuse in stepfamilies, medical personnel may be more inclined to attribute injuries of stepchildren to abuse than injuries of children in first married families.

Although empirical studies offer limited and sometimes conflict-ing results about the prevalence of child abuse in stepfamilies, theories about child abuse in stepfamilies abound. Kalmuss and Seltzer (1989) proposed a *family socialization framework* that suggests three reasons why family violence is more likely in remarried households than in first marriages. First, at least some individuals in remarried families are more likely to have been socialized to patterns of family conflict and violence in their previous family units (Giles-Sims & Finkelhor, 1984). Second, characteristics of postdivorce remarried households (e.g., complexity, lack of institutional support, role ambiguity) may increase the likelihood of conflict and violence. Third, at least some members of remarried households have experienced the cumulative stress of multiple family transitions that often is related to family conflict and violence. *Family socialization theory,* loosely based on social learning theory, would predict that characteristics of families containing divorced and remarried individuals make conflict more probable, but certainly not inevitable. *Social learning theory* might predict that men are more likely to abuse children because they are not socialized to learn how to care for children and have very little exposure to good child care role models (Margolin, 1992).

Giles-Sims and Finkelhor (1984) offered five theories of child physical abuse and child sexual abuse in stepfamilies, phenomena with potentially different causes. The five theories are social-evolutionary or sociobiological, normative, stress, selection, and resource.

Social-evolutionary theory predicts that physical abuse of stepchildren is likely to occur because stepparents have a lesser investment in children who do not carry their genes. The principle of *natural selection* inclines males and females to invest only in their own offspring and to "avoid squandering valuable reproductive effort on someone else's offspring" (Daly & Wilson, 1980, p. 279). Females become attached readily to their infants, a mechanism that helps ensure that their efforts will foster the survival of their children. Because paternity is more difficult to prove than maternity, men attempt to control the sex lives of their female partners in order to increase the probability that the offspring are genetically their own (Daly & Wilson, 1980; Fisher, 1989). The sociobiological perspective argues that stepchildren are at risk because of the evolutionary tendency of parents to protect their own reproductive efforts and not those of others. Just as animals attack and kill the offspring of others so that their offspring might have a better chance of survival, so may stepparents abuse those who are not the product of their reproductive efforts.

Social-evolutionary theory posits that because inbreeding reduces fitness, sexual relations with offspring are taboo. Stepchildren are at risk for sexual abuse by their stepparents because the incest taboo does not apply to them. Wilson and Daly (1987) even argued that "children's extreme dislike of discord between their natural parents and their alarm at the prospect of parental remarriage reflect a remarkably astute assessment of their own best interests, and may even be adaptive emotional responses that have been specifically favored in our natural selective history" (p. 227).

Giles-Sims and Finkelhor (1984) are not enthusiastic about social-evolutionary theory. They noted that the theory does not explain the often-reported physical and sexual abuse of biological children by their parents, nor does much empirical evidence support the theoretical propositions suggested.

Somewhat congruent with social-evolutionary theory, *normative theory* attributes the higher rates of sexual abuse by stepfathers to the fact that nonblood relatives are less subject to normative taboos against incest. Normative theory is supported at least partially by the legal system in that marriage between stepkin is legal in many states. However, empirical evidence to support this theory is lacking. In fact, although normative theory would predict that the most taboo form of incest would be that between father and daughter, father-daughter incest is much more common than mother-son incest. Normative theory also does not explain why nonnatal British fathers (stepfathers and cohabiting fathers) were more likely to abuse stepchildren but less likely than biological fathers to subject victims to intercourse (Gordon & Creighton, 1988).

Stress theory posits that stepchild abuse is related to the higher levels of stress in stepfamilies. According to Giles-Sims and Finkelhor (1984), stress theory has theoretical and empirical support and accounts for more of the correlates of child abuse than either social-evolutionary or normative theory. For example, empirical evidence from the National Survey of Violence in American Families (Straus, Gelles, & Steinmetz, 1980) links stress to child abuse. It is also well documented that stepfamilies experience stress (Crosbie-

Burnett, 1989a). The cumulative stress that may result from the multiple family transitions associated with remarriage increases the risk of abuse (Kalmuss & Seltzer, 1989), as perhaps does the absence of institutional support and norms for stepparents (Cherlin, 1978). What is not known is how some stepfamilies manage to reduce or control stress, and whether reducing stress also reduces child abuse in stepfamilies.

Selection theory, as posited by Giles-Sims and Finkelhor (1984) suggests that the association between stepfamilies and child abuse is due to conditions common to both. For example, stepfamilies may have a higher proportion of members who have individual predispositions toward violence than other families. It may have been these personality characteristics predisposing them toward violence that precipitated the breakup of relationships prior to the remarriage. The pool of remarried individuals, therefore, might contain a higher percentage of people prone to violence than a pool of individuals in first marriages. No empirical evidence supports this theory, and critics would say that the theory ignores the fact that divorce and remarriage often result from a desire for a better family life.

Resource theory predicts that the more resources a person has (e.g., money, power, education, parenting skills), the less likely it is that he or she will have to resort to physical force to get his or her way. However, even when stepfathers bring numerous resources to the stepfamily household, their authority may be questioned by the stepchildren and often the mother as well. Resource theory would suggest that the stepfather then might resort to physical abuse to gain authority.

The theories discussed here point out numerous explanations for the possible occurrence of child abuse in stepfamilies. However, none of them have been tested adequately. Crosbie-Burnett (1989a) proposed using the double ABCX model to test family stress theory and to assess and help stepfamilies. This model also could be a test of resource theory. However promising these efforts to test the theories of child abuse in stepfamilies, it is probably true that cultural stereotypes, lack of comparability across research designs, inaccurate reporting of data, and the private nature of family interaction in American households will continue to impede the advancement of knowledge in this important area.

5

Other Stepfamily Relationships

The previous chapter was devoted to the important stepparent-stepchild bond, often considered to be a key to close relationships in remarried families. In this chapter we focus on other important, but less frequently studied, stepfamily relationships. We begin with a discussion of the relationship between parents and children after either one or both parents remarry. Residential parent-child relationships are presented first, followed by a section on nonresidential parents and their children. The focus of the residential parent-child section is on mothers primarily, and the nonresidential parent section examines research mainly on father-child relationships. These emphases reflect the fact that after divorce it is relatively rare for fathers to have physical custody of their children. The next section of the chapter presents a discussion of siblings, stepsiblings, and half-siblings, relationships that are only beginning to receive attention by researchers.

Information about interactions between former spouses and a discussion of the normative beliefs about how former spouses should relate after divorce and remarriage are presented next. The final two sections of the chapter are devoted to the roles of grandparents and stepgrandparents in the remarried family. Any and all of these relationships can be emotionally close and important to the well functioning of remarried families. None have been investigated thoroughly.

✿ Parent-Child Relationships

Residential Parents and Their Children

The relationship between the residential parent and his or her child is often the closest family bond at the beginning of the stepfamily, even closer than the remarried couple. The relatively greater closeness of this relationship in the early stages of remarried family life is not unusual; the bonds between parents and children predate the remarried family household, and parents and their children have shared many family experiences prior to the onset of remarried family life that are likely to strengthen the ties between them (see Chapter 6 for the clinical view of these issues).

The parent-child relationship in remarried family households is potentially an extremely important one; parents are legally responsible for their children, they are emotionally invested in the children, and there is a biological connection, except in the case of adoption. Along with the stepparent, biological parents and children constitute the triad whose interactions serve as the bases for many stepfamily difficulties. However, despite the potential significance of the residential parent-child relationship, it is less often the primary focus of empirical studies than is the stepparent-stepchild relationship, perhaps because the latter association is viewed as more problematic and therefore of more urgent concern.

Prior to the mid-1980s, research on the relationship between remarried parents and their children was limited both in design and in the scope of topics addressed. For example, it was common for researchers to compare the degree of perceived emotional closeness between parents and children in remarried families to parent-child closeness in other family structures and to stepparent-child affection (cf. Bowerman & Irish, 1962; Fox & Inazu, 1982; Halperin & Smith, 1983). Not surprisingly, children generally felt more attachment to parents than to stepparents, and closer to mothers than to fathers. However, seldom were differences found in feelings of closeness to residential biological parents in different family structures (Coleman & Ganong, 1990); that is, children felt similarly close to residential biological mothers whether they lived in first marriage families, single-parent households, or stepfather family households. With rare exceptions (e.g., Santrock, Warshak, Lindbergh, & Meadows, 1982) these studies were based on self-report data gathered from one family member only, usually the child; all were cross-sectional designs. Researchers oversimplified stepfamily complexity. Variations in stepfamily structure most often were ignored, and potential moderating variables, such as the number of years since the parent's remarriage, frequently were not assessed. In general, studies of the emotional attachments between parents and children in remarried families used such simple designs and underconceptualizations of remarried family life that results shed little light on the dynamics of these relationships.

Recent studies have been more complex in design, and researchers often have attempted to frame their work within the context of more sophisticated understandings of how stepfamilies function. For example Anderson and White (1986) hypothesized that (a) mother-child coalitions would be stronger in stepfather households than in nuclear families and (b) dysfunctional stepfamilies would have stronger mother-child coalitions than functional stepfamilies. Both of these hypotheses were supported in a comparative study of functional and dysfunctional nuclear families and stepfamilies. These predictions were based partly on the belief that relationships in stepfamilies are somewhat different from those in nuclear families but that differences per se do not mean stepfamilies are inherently dysfunctional (Anderson & White, 1986; Brown et al., 1990). Healthy nuclear families do not encourage coalitions between one parent and a child to the relative exclusion of the other parent. Such coalitions have been seen as an indication of marital problems or widespread family problems (Minuchin, 1974). In well-functioning stepfamilies, however, it may be normative for the biological parent and child to form an alliance, if it is not too extreme.

What is needed to clarify the connection between parent-child closeness and overall family functioning are longitudinal studies that examine how these relationships function in different family structures. A major investigation that meets this description was conducted by Hetherington, Clingempeel, and associates (Hetherington & Clingempeel, 1992). They studied relationships between mothers and preadolescent children over time in newly formed remarried (stepfather) families, nondivorced nuclear families, and postdivorced mother-headed families. This study, to date, has provided the most comprehensive data on residential parent-child relationships. Among their findings are the following:

- Initially, mother-child relationships in stepfamilies deteriorated.
- Children in stepfamilies were more negative toward their mothers initially, but by 26 months after the remarriage, the mother-child relationship in stepfamilies was very similar to the mother-child relationship in nondivorced families.
- Mothers in stepfamilies monitored the behavior of both sons and daughters less than nondivorced and divorced mothers during the first year of remarriage, but over time their behavior became more similar to that of nondivorced mothers.
- Observers reported that during the early months of remarriage, children displayed higher levels of antisocial behavior to their mother and stepfather. However, neither the children nor their teachers perceived children in stepfamilies as having more problems than children in nondivorced families.
- Remarried mothers, in general, were less involved than divorced mothers in their children's lives.
- Observed interactions between children and their remarried mothers were less positive than mother-child interactions in the other family forms.
- Although children in all three family types showed increasingly negative behavior as they entered adolescence, they eventually became more positive to all parents except stepfathers, as their parents became less emotionally involved and granted them greater autonomy.

In another longitudinal study of remarried families, Bray and colleagues (Bray et al., 1987) examined the parenting styles of mothers in stepfather families and found that newly remarried mothers of 6- to 8-year-old children engaged in more *authoritarian* parenting, while first-marriage mothers were more *authoritative*. This finding means that remarried mothers were more likely to use stern, dogmatic control without explaining the reasons for their discipline to children, whereas mothers in nuclear families were more likely to control their children's behavior by using warmth and logical explanations for their rules. The researchers speculated that newly remarried mothers were compensating for the more *permissive* style of discipline engaged in by the stepfathers. If so, it could be hypothesized that, over time, remarried mothers' parenting styles would become more like those of mothers in first marriages, providing that stepfathers began to assume more disciplinary duties.

In contrast to Bray et al.'s findings, but consistent with those of Hetherington and Clingempeel, Kurdek and Fine (1993) found that adolescents in stepfather family households reported more permissive parenting than did those living with stepmothers. These results suggest that developmental factors must be considered in drawing conclusions regarding residential parents and children, factors related to both the age of the children and the developmental state of the stepfamily.

Relationships are not static. They change as children and adults get older, they change in response to other family alterations (e.g., birth of another child, a stepsibling moving into the residence), and they change in response to developmental modifications in other close relationships. For example a newly remarried mother's early preoccupation with a new spouse may create feelings of jealousy or insecurity in her children. They may withdraw from her, turning to their nonresidential parent, to grandparents, to siblings, or to nonrelatives for nurture and support. Or they may create conflicts with the stepfather, in hopes of forcing their mother to choose sides. Or they may misbehave in school or act out in other ways that demand the mother's attention. We also could hypothesize a scenario in which children welcome the emotional distance and interpersonal freedom they experience when their mother remarries. In this scenario the mother-child relationship becomes more satisfying to both participants following remarriage.

Hetherington, Clingempeel, and colleagues reported considerable diversity in the remarried mother-child relationships they studied. In-depth, qualitative studies perhaps could enlighten us about differences in remarried parent-child relationships between families and across time, as well as about the consequences of these differences. Obviously many moderating and mediating variables are involved in predicting the dynamics of residential parent-child ties in remarried families.

Nonresidential Parents and Their Children

The Census Bureau (U.S. Bureau of the Census, 1992) reported that single-parent households headed by fathers increased from 2.1% in 1980 to 4.9% in 1990. Much of the increase has been attributed to joint legal custody arrangements that include shared physical custody of some sort (Miller & Schreiner, 1992). Therefore, although there are nonresidential biological mothers, the vast majority of nonresidential parents are fathers, and we focus on them in this section.

Although there is a growing body of research on nonresidential parenting after divorce (Bray & Depner, 1993), far less attention has been paid to what happens to nonresidential parent-child relationships when one or both biological parents remarry. Recently Braver, Wolchik, Sandler, and Sheets (1993) used a social exchange model to theorize about the nonresidential parent-child relationship in remarried families.

Braver et al. (1993) hypothesized that the greater the perceived rewards and the fewer the perceived costs of the parent-child relationship, the greater the parental involvement will be. More specifically, they propose that as the affectional/interpersonal, material/tangible, and symbolic/moral rewards increase, the nonresidential parent's involvement with the child should increase, leading to more visitation and better child-support compliance. The factors in the social exchange model developed by Braver et al. are displayed on Table 5.1.

Table 5.1 The Factors in the Social Exchange Model Predicted to Impact Nonresidential Parent's Involvement With the Child

---

Affectional or Interpersonal Costs
- Visitation experienced as awkward, stressful, disturbing, or unpleasant.
- Limited relationship to the child and family is regarded by the nonresidential parent as painful.
- Anger at the ex-spouse.
- Conflict with the ex-spouse.
- Denigration by the ex-spouse.
- Visitation discouraged, interfered with, prevented, or threatened by the residential parent.
- Relationship with child interferes with or prevents interaction in other enjoyable interpersonal relationships, such as with friends or family.
- Relationship with the child interferes with interaction with a new partner or spouse, or new children or stepchildren.
- If the new partner opposes or is irritated by the relationship between the nonresidential parent and child.
- If there is friction between the new partner and a child.
- If there is friction between the child and new children introduced as the result of new romantic relationships.

Affectional or Interpersonal Rewards
- Visitation relieves loneliness.
- Visiting relationship regarded as beneficial for the child.
- Relationship supported by significant other such as important family and friends.

Material or Tangible Costs
- Perceived or actual privation or economic hardship of meeting the child support obligation.
- The financial costs of visitation.
- The competing nonsocial time demands on the nonresidential parent, such as work demands and household tasks.

Material or Tangible Rewards
- The perceived costs in time and money of discontinuing child support.

Symbolic or Moral Costs
- Child support is thought to be misused by the residential parent (is using money for self).
- Child support obligation considered to be unfair.
- Dissatisfied with the divorce settlement (e.g., property settlement, custody arrangement), or divorce system considered to be unfair.
- Nonresidential parent's lack of control over aspects of the post-divorce relationship with the child.

Symbolic or Moral Rewards
- Symbolic commitment to the parent role.
- Guilt over marital disruption.
- Moral obligation to honor agreements.

SOURCE: From "A Social Exchange Model of Nonresidential Parent Involvement" by S. L. Braver, S. A. Wolchik, I. N. Sandler, and V. L. Sheets, 1993, in *Nonresidential Parenting: New Vistas in Family Living*, C. Depner & J. Bray (Eds.), pp. 94-95. Copyright © 1993 by Sage.

Affectional or Interpersonal Costs. Stress associated with visiting children, the first "cost" mentioned in their model, may increase after the custodial parent remarries. Many fathers disengage from their children soon after the divorce because they feel awkward about visiting their children and/or having the children visit them and because seeing the children is too emotionally painful (Furstenberg, 1987). The pain may increase if the father perceives that the stepfather is taking over his parenting role. Some nonresidential fathers may feel that they no longer have much to offer their children in the way of a role model. Feeling displaced may greatly increase the costs of maintaining the relationship.

Anger at, conflict with, and denigration by the ex-spouse may accelerate after a former partner has remarried. If the nonresidential father remarries, the mother may be jealous, feel rejected, and begin to worry about the continuance of child support. She may be worried also that the stepmother will compete with her for the children's love and loyalty. These insecurities may manifest themselves in hostile, unpleasant ways that damage the relationships between all of the parental figures and the children. If the mother's hostility toward the stepmother spills over to the children's behavior, the father may have to weigh the benefits of continuing to have a close relationship with his children against the costs of developing and maintaining a close relationship with his new wife.

If the mother remarries and her family fantasy includes duplicating the nuclear family model, she may try to replace the children's father with the new stepfather by actively discouraging contacts between the children and their biological father. If she makes visits uncertain and unstable or is hostile about making visitation arrangements, the costs of trying to maintain regular visits with the children may be no longer worth the effort to the father. He already may feel that his role with the children is being usurped; fighting over visitation could cause him to withdraw completely from the situation.

Material or Tangible Costs. Material or tangible costs to the father are not likely to change much after the mother remarries. If the father remarries, however, he may be taking on new financial responsibilities for stepchildren who now may be living with him.

He may perceive that he no longer is able to afford traveling to see his children or paying for transportation for them to visit him if they live some distance away from him. His new wife may resent money leaving the household to help support his children who live elsewhere. This resentment may be especially true if she works outside the home and perceives that some of her income is going toward supporting her husband's ex-wife. Recent legislation has made it more difficult for parents to avoid paying child support, but many fathers provide additional discretionary financial support as well (e.g., travel funds for visits, gifts, vacations, music lessons). This outlay of money may especially anger the new wife, the children will be resentful if they no longer receive these "rewards" from their father, and the father may respond to the discomfort by cutting off visits with his children.

Symbolic or Moral Costs. The symbolic or moral costs of visitation also may change after remarriage. Fathers who felt guilt over the marital disruption may feel less guilty once the ex-wife remarries. If guilt was the driving force behind his involvement with his children, he may become less involved. His commitment to parenting his nonresidential biological children may lessen when he has shared children with his new wife or when he acquires residential stepchildren through remarriage. The costs of maintaining multiple fathering roles are too much for some men; the tendency is to maintain the father role in his household and to withdraw from attempting to father his nonresidential children.

It is noteworthy that even in nonindustrialized cultures, many of these patterns prevail. For example, Flinn (1992) reported that men in a rural village in north-central Trinidad interacted less frequently with their nonresidential children after acquiring a new mate. They also interacted less frequently with their children from previous mating relationships if their ex-spouses had acquired new mates.

The notion that the interaction of children with their nonresidential parents will affect positively the children's development is intuitively appealing but has little empirical support (Emery, 1988; Furstenberg & Cherlin, 1991). It is equally logical to expect that frequent contacts will have positive effects for nonresidential parents, but this has not been examined empirically for remarried nonresidential parents. It is tempting to try to draw conclusions about nonresidential parent-child bonds in remarried families from the literature on postdivorce, nonremarried parents. However, the addition of one or more stepparents, and perhaps stepsiblings and other stepkin, undoubtedly has a substantial effect on the dynamics of the nonresidential parent-child relationships. The connection between nonresidential parents and children, in turn, also could have profound effects on other remarried family ties (e.g., remarriage, stepparent-stepchild, stepsiblings). Rather than generalize about this relationship from data collected from nonremarried families, researchers should design studies specifically focusing on nonresidential parents in remarried families by using the Braver et al. (1993) or other theoretical models.

❧ Siblings, Stepsiblings, and Half-Siblings

Underlying much of the research on the effects of living in a stepfamily on children are one of two assumptions: (a) Children's emotional and behavioral adjustment to stepfamily living is a function of marital conflict or other marital problems (Coleman & Ganong, 1987b), and (b) children's adjustment is a consequence of the stepparent-stepchild relationship (Coleman & Ganong, 1990; Ganong & Coleman, 1986). Rosenberg and Hajfal (1985) argued that these assumptions imply a *dripolator effect*, in which influences from the top of the stepfamily system filter down to the bottom. They suggest there also may be *percolator effects* in stepfamilies, wherein influences from relationships at the bottom bubble to the top, resulting in either negative or positive effects on the family. A major source of these percolator effects is the relationships between children in remarried families.

In stepfamilies, children often acquire stepsiblings and, eventually, half-siblings, in addition to the brothers and sisters they may have had prior to the remarriage. To further add to the complexity, children may reside either full-time or part-time with any combination of siblings, stepsiblings, and half-siblings, or they may not live with them at all.

Data on the prevalence of step- and half-siblings are difficult to acquire. Most data on these relationships are obtained from studies that were not specifically designed to garner this information. The best estimations are that approximately three-fourths of the children who reside with a remarried parent have at least one sibling and that nearly one-fifth have a half-sibling (Bumpass, 1984), usually acquired within the first few years after stepfamily formation (Wineberg, 1990, 1992). The number of stepsiblings is not known. Approximately 1 out of 15 stepfamily households is complex (Sweet, 1991), meaning both adults have children from prior relationships living in the household, but this underestimates the number of stepsiblings because it does not count non-residential stepsiblings.

Before we discuss what is known about the relationships between children in remarried families, we should define what we mean by siblings, half-siblings, and stepsiblings. We use the term *siblings* to refer to children who are biologically related to the same mother and father. These genetically related brothers and sisters are also sometimes called *full siblings* or *biological siblings* in the literature. Sibling relationships also exist when children have been adopted by the same two parents.

The distinction between half-siblings and full siblings is not clear to many people. A *half-sibling relationship* is present when two or more children share a biological (or adoptive) connection to one, but not both, parents. For example President Bill Clinton and Roger Clinton are half-brothers because they have the same mother but different fathers (Roger's father was Bill's stepfather, and Bill's father was his mother's first husband). President Clinton allegedly may have another half-brother, a man from California, because they have the same father but different mothers. It is possible, as in this example, for a person to have half-siblings that are unrelated to each other (Roger Clinton is unrelated to the man from California).

Stepsiblings are not biologically or legally related to each other. For example when a man with children from a previous relationship remarries a woman with children from a previous relationship, the new husband's children become stepsiblings to the new wife's children. Stepsiblings are always part of complex stepfamilies because two stepparents are in the family. The households in which they live, however, may contain only the father's children or only the mother's children.

Siblings. In general, relationships between siblings have received less attention from scholars than other important family bonds. Although researchers recently have shown a growing interest in sibling relationships (Boer & Dunn, 1992; Zukow, 1989), little of this interest has been extended to research about biological siblings in stepfamilies. A few years ago, Ihinger-Tallman (1987) outlined several propositions concerning how and why sibling (and stepsibling) bonds develop or fail to develop in postdivorce remarried families, but these propositions remain to be tested.

When researchers have focused on sibling relationships in remarried families, they frequently have aggregated full, half-, and step-siblings into one group (Amato, 1987; Ferri, 1984), making it impossible to assess the unique dynamics of each type. Combining these types of children's relationships together also makes it impossible to determine how relationships between siblings in remarried families differ from those of stepsiblings and half-siblings.

The few studies that have examined sibling relationships in remarried families indicate that they are less close than sibling relationships in other family types (Anderson & Rice, 1992; White & Reidmann, 1992). As part of the Virginia Longitudinal Study of Divorce and Remarriage (Hetherington & Clingempeel, 1992), Anderson and Rice (1992) assessed changes in the quality and functioning of sibling relationships over a 2 ½-year period in newly remarried families, divorced maternal custody families, and nondivorced families. In addition to asking mothers, fathers, and target children (ages 9-13 at the beginning of the study) about sibling relationships, sibling interactions were observed in a play situation, in a family problem-solving situation, and at the dinner table. According to all family members, boys in remarried families were less supportive and more negative to siblings than boys and girls from other families. Girls in remarried families, however, did not significantly differ from other girls, and even offered more support to siblings during the first year of parental remarriage. Observations indicated that sibling interactions in divorced families were more negative than in stepfamilies or married families, but sibling relationships in stepfamilies became more negative over time.

Although children from all three family types increasingly disengaged from their siblings as they entered adolescence, the transition to parental remarriage seemed to have accelerated this normative process (Anderson & Rice, 1992). Rather than bonding together in the face of parental remarriage, siblings disengaged from each other. This sibling disengagement in stepfamilies may carry over into adulthood; White and Reidmann (1992), using data collected in the National Survey of Families and Households, found that siblings who were part of a remarried family prior to age 18 had slightly less contact as adults than siblings whose parents remained married during their childhood years. They attributed the difference to "stepfamily dynamics" (p. 206), presumably related to stressful interactions. Anderson and Rice (1992) speculated that children in remarried families had more negative and less positive interactions with siblings as a result of stresses they were experiencing due to their parent's relatively recent remarriage, but it could be that these patterns of interaction continue for years.

The lack of attention paid to sibling relationships in remarried families is unfortunate because sibling relationships can be extremely important to an individual's psychological and behavioral development (Boer & Dunn, 1992; Cicirelli, in press; Hoffman, 1991). It is believed that siblings perform several important functions for each other, among them identity formation, protection from parents and others, mutual regulation of behavior, socialization, support, and the exchange of direct services, such as lending money or giving rides (Bank & Kahn, 1982). If siblings disengage from each other after remarriage, do they continue to perform these functions for each other? If not, how and why are sibling relationships in remarried families different from those in other family types? If increased stress within the stepfamily affects siblings, what are the mechanisms by which greater stress changes sibling dynamics? These and other questions remain to be answered.

Half-Siblings. Beer (1992) identified three types of half-siblings: visiting outsiders, resident outsiders, and resident insiders. In this schema the child born to the remarried adults is the *resident insider* because he or she is related to both adults in the household. The mutual child and the parents can be thought of as forming a nuclear family unit within a stepfamily; hence older half-siblings are outsiders to this nuclear unit. The stepchildren are the outsiders, because they are related to only one of the parents, and they either reside with their half-sibling (*resident outsider*) or not (*visiting outsider*).

How well do half-siblings get along? Bernstein (1989), in a qualitative study of remarried families who had reproduced, found that relationships were better when there were larger age differences between half-siblings, when the remarried family had been together longer, when half-siblings lived together, and when children were similar in temperament.

Half-siblings who live together all or most of the time generally think of each other simply as siblings (Bernstein, 1989; Ganong & Coleman, 1988). The "half" is a meaningless abstraction, and they do not refer to each other as half-brothers or half-sisters. When children have little contact, however, distinctions between half-siblings and full siblings are more common; in these situations the "sibling" part of the label "half-sibling" is the meaningless abstraction (Bernstein, 1989). Unfortunately, not enough is known about half-sibling relationships to conclude whether they function similarly to those of siblings or not or, if so, under what conditions.

Considerably more interest has been shown on the percolator effects of half-sibling relationships on other family relationships than on studying half-sibling bonds per se. The rationale is that because a child born to the remarried couple is related biologically to everyone else in the stepfamily household, this shared biological connection will help facilitate integration as a family unit and will draw the marital dyad and steprelationships (e.g., stepparent-stepchild, stepsiblings) closer (Ganong & Coleman, 1988).

Several years ago we jokingly referred to our study of childbearing in stepfamilies as our "concrete baby study" because it was inspired partly by stepfamily self-help books that proclaimed having a child together would help "cement" family bonds. Although the assertion was not empirically supported in our assessment of responses on standardized measures of relationship closeness and quality, parents who had reproduced in the remarriage nonetheless perceived that there were benefits of having a child together (Ganong & Coleman, 1988), as did parents in Bernstein's (1989) study, who felt that the baby provided "a reason to ride out the rough times" (p. 89). However, there were indications that mutual children were sources of stress as well.

Research findings on the effects of mutual children on other family relationships are generally mixed. For example, investigators found that the presence of a half-sibling negatively affected the stepmother-stepchild relationship (Ambert, 1986; Santrock & Sitterle, 1987), positively affected the stepfather-child relationship (Ambert, 1986; Hobart, 1988), was not related to stepmother-stepchild ties (Ahrons & Wallisch, 1987; Ganong & Coleman, 1988; Hobart, 1988), had little effect on stepfamily relations (Ahrons & Wallisch, 1987; Booth et al., 1984; Ganong & Coleman, 1988), had a negative influence on older children's behavior (Zill, 1988), and reduced the amount of time mothers had to spend with their children from prior marriages (Ahrons & Wallisch, 1987). Some of these discrepant results may be explained by differences in the timing of the assessment; half-sibling relations may be more stress-producing when children are younger (Bernstein, 1989; Ganong & Coleman, 1988). Researchers generally have not examined potential moderator variables that could be influencing the effects of half-siblings on other family relationships (e.g., age differences, gender combinations, amount of contact). In addition to these structural variables, unexamined intrapersonal variables such as temperament, expectations, and reasons for reproducing in remarriage potentially are factors in determining the quality of half-sibling relationships, as well as the effect the mutual child has on other relationships. Most of the studies simply investigated the presence/absence of a half-sibling in a family as the sole predictor of other outcome variables.

Information about half-siblings could have important implications, especially for those stepfamilies most likely to reproduce: younger, postdivorce stepfamilies in which one of the adults has not been married before or has not had children prior to the marriage (Bernstein, 1989; Ganong & Coleman, 1988). Despite inconclusive evidence regarding the "concrete baby effect," adults in remarried families continue to have children partly in order to strengthen stepfamily bonds.

Stepsiblings. The existence of stepsiblings in a family means that both adults probably have been married at least once before. Consequently, everything may double: There may be at least two living former spouses, two sets of extended former kin, and children in the remarried family may reside periodically in two other households. The family has two stepparents, because each adult partner is a stepparent, as well as a parent.

If two sets of children will be living together all or most of the time, remarried families may have to move into housing large enough to accommodate both sets of children. Accompanying such moves may be shifts into new schools, loss of friends and the familiarity of the old neighborhoods, and a host of other stressors to be added to the transition into remarried family life. If one set of children or some children from both sets live most of the time elsewhere (e.g., with their other parent), then efforts still have to be made to accommodate/incorporate the nonresidential children into the stepfamily household for visits or extended stays.

When there are stepsibling relationships, there are also many challenges, among them financial, interpersonal, and residential complications. When two parents combine their offspring, lifestyle changes for children are highly probable. As we have seen with other dimensions of remarried family life, researchers and clinicians generally have associated increased complexity with increased problems, and stepsibling relationships in complex stepfamilies are no exception. Clinicians have identified a number of potential difficulties in stepsibling relationships: sibling rivalry, competition over scarce resources such as parental attention and space, sexual attraction, having little in common, changes in family size, and changes in the child's position in the family (Rosenberg & Hajfal, 1985; Walsh, 1992).

Only a handful of researchers have examined the relationship between stepsiblings (Beer, 1992; Duberman, 1975; Ganong & Coleman, 1987; White & Reidmann, 1992). In the eyes of parents and stepparents, stepsiblings get along well with each other (Duberman, 1975; Ganong & Coleman, in press) although many remarried adults recognize periodic conflict. In an in-depth study of 52 complex stepfamilies, 39% of the adults perceived "normal" sibling rivalry between stepsiblings, 33% saw jealousy, 12% reported that sharing space was a problem, 12% thought that their children had nothing in common with their stepsiblings, and 4% identified competition as a source of trouble in stepsibling relationships (Ganong & Coleman, in press).

In general, stepsibling relationships are not as close as sibling relationships, both during childhood (Ganong & Coleman, in press) and in adulthood (White & Reidmann, 1992). This is not to suggest that stepsiblings' interactions are negative and hostile; on the contrary, stepsibling relationships were reported to be characterized by generally positive affect (Ganong & Coleman, in press) and substantial contact in adulthood (White & Reidmann, 1992).

Ihinger-Tallman (1987) speculated that there are normative pressures on stepsiblings to hold affectionate feelings for each other. She also hypothesized that stepsiblings were more likely to bond:

- if they have frequent contact
- if they share experiences
- if conditions foster intimacy (freedom to express emotions and a lack of competition for resources) and interdependency (exchanges of rewards between stepsiblings)
- if they are similar in age, gender, experiences, and values; if there are few perceived costs and more perceived benefits to associating together
- if there is perceived equality in giving up aspects of their premarriage lifestyle

To date, these speculations have not triggered much interest by researchers.

In summary, a number of questions remain to be answered or at least to be answered fully about the relationships between children in stepfamilies. For example:

- What is the nature of stepsibling and half-sibling bonds?
- Are stepsiblings considered to be "real" kin?
- Do children in remarried families make distinctions between siblings, half-siblings, and stepsiblings?

- What effects do stepsiblings have on each other?
- Do stepsiblings provide stress-buffering effects, or do they increase stress related to parental remarriage?
- Do half-siblings strengthen emotional ties in the stepfamily?
- Are there sex differences in adaptation to stepsiblings?
- How are half-sibling and stepsibling relationships related to developmental changes in children?

The notion of percolator effects in stepfamilies holds intuitive appeal. The relationships between children in stepfamilies, and the effects of these relationships on other family relationships, should be fruitful areas of inquiry in the future. Researchers interested in the close relationships between children in remarried families should examine the growing literature on sibling relationships in nuclear families for conceptual and methodological ideas.

ʲ Former Spouse Relationships

Generally, when former spouse relationships in remarried families are maintained, it is for the purpose of coparenting children. In postdivorce families in which nonresidential parents have little contact with their children after the divorce, former spouse relationships are virtually nonexistent. Nonetheless, for at least half, and perhaps for the majority of divorced persons, former spouses interact with each other at least occasionally (Ambert, 1989; Hobart, 1989). Obviously, a former spouse relationship does not exist when a partner has died, at least not in the same sense as in postdivorce remarried families. In Chapter 4 we discussed the coparenting dimension of former spouse relationships, so in this chapter we broaden our examination of former spouse relationships.

There is a great deal of diversity in how former spouses interact. The research by Ahrons on former spouse relationships, described at some length in Chapter 2, clearly illustrates that the dynamics of such relationships vary widely (Ahrons & Rodgers, 1987). Ambert (1989), in a longitudinal, in-depth study of former spouses and current spouses, categorized former spouse relationships as friendly, angry, or indifferent.

Similarly, Giles-Sims (1987a) developed a typology of former spouse relationships in remarried families based on two dimensions: the degree to which resources are shared between former spouses, and the quality of affect in the relationship between former spouses. Although her results are based on a small sample, they offer additional insights into the diversity of former spouse relationships. Resource sharing was assessed with three variables: (a) the amount of contact with the former spouse, (b) the degree to which the former spouse was consulted on decisions regarding the children, and (c) the receipt of child support. The quality of affect was measured by asking the remarried adults how satisfied they were with the parenting relationship they had with their former spouse.

These two dimensions resulted in a four-category typology. The *cooperative* category identified ex-spouses who shared resources and had satisfying coparental relationships that were characterized by positive affect. Children had frequent and regular contact with their nonresidential parent, and mutual parenting was basically cooperative. The *hostile* group interacted with the former spouse, and children saw their nonresidential parent frequently; interactions with the former spouse, however, were often acrimonious. The hostile relationship between the former spouses demanded a lot of time and energy and often presented problems for the stepfamily. In the *indifferent* or *relieved* category, contact with the former spouse was infrequent, and the response of the remarried partner was one of relief that the former spouse was not involved. Presumably the former spouse relationship had been characterized by conflicts or the divorce was a hostile one, because the remarried adults anticipated conflict and disruption to their routines if the former spouse was to participate in decisions regarding the child. In these families, stepparents actively replaced the former spouse in parenting. The *resentful* group had little or no involvement with their former spouses, but instead of being grateful, these remarried adults were resentful that child support was not being paid and/or that the children were abandoned. In some of these families the stepparent assumed the parental responsibilities of the absent parent, but in others they did not, perhaps contributing to the anger and resentment felt by the biological parent.

Giles-Sims (1987a) found that these types of former spouse relationships were related to stepfamily functioning. Stepfamilies with cooperative former spouse relationships had greater cohesion, more open expression, and less conflict than other types. On the other extreme, the hostiles had less cohesion, less expressiveness, and more conflict than others. Although the direction of effects cannot be determined from this cross-sectional, correlational study (i.e., did the type of relationships with former spouses affect stepfamily interactions, or did better stepfamily functioning lead to better former spouse ties?), it is probable that stepfamily interactions were influenced more by the nature of the former spouse bonds than vice versa, because the patterns of former spouse interactions were established prior to the formation of the stepfamily.

This is not to suggest that remarriages do not alter former spouse relationships. In fact, remarriages may trigger many changes in how former spouses interact. (See Chapter 4 for hypothesized changes that revolve around children's issues [e.g., custody, visitation, child support].) Unfortunately, relatively little research has been conducted on former spouse relationships in remarried families (cf. Ahrons & Rodgers, 1987; Ambert, 1989; Giles-Sims, 1987a), so it is difficult to draw many conclusions about these relationships. It is known that former spouses often are evaluated quite negatively by remarried former partners and their new spouses (Guisinger et al., 1989; Hobart, 1989).

Research on the impact of the relationship with former spouses on remarriage has yielded mixed results. For example, Clingempeel (1981) found a curvilinear relationship between the frequency of contacts with former spouses and remarital quality: Those with moderate amounts of contact with their former spouses reported higher remarital quality than those with low or high amounts of contact. In a partial replication of this study, however, Clingempeel and Brand (1985) found no relationship between former spouses' contact and remarriage satisfaction. Simply measuring the frequency of contact between former spouses may not be sufficient to assess the impact of former spouses on remarriage functioning. Weston and Macklin (1990) found that the relation between contact with a former spouse and remarriage functioning was moderated by other factors, such as the degree to which former spouses cooperate on parenting, and the congruence between the kind of former spouse relationship that exists and ideal expectations for such a relationship. The amount of contact between former spouses actually may reveal little about the nature of those relationships or about the effects of former spouses on remarriages; couples who communicate and compromise with each other may have a great deal of contact, as might couples who hate each other but are in frequent contact in order to fight more about the children. In this first situation the former spouse may serve as a source of social support for the remarried couple; in the second situation the former spouse may be a source of greater stress on the remarriage relationship (Weston & Macklin, 1990). In a study of remarried fathers and their new wives, the men's former spouses were a greater source of stress on the remarried couples than were the stepchildren, and negative perceptions of the husband's former spouse were related positively to remarital satisfaction for both husbands and wives (Guisinger et al., 1989). Clinicians have pointed out that former spouse relationships are important for predicting overall family functioning, and they have identified several questions that researchers could study (Ahrons, 1980).

Normative Beliefs
About Former Spouse Relationships

Are there culturally agreed-on expectations for how former spouses should interact with each other? As in other relationships in remarried families, researchers have pointed out that there are no institutionalized norms concerning this relationship (Burgoyne & Clark, 1984; Goode, 1956). Goetting (1979) attempted to determine whether remarried adults could identify consensually held beliefs about how former spouse relationships should be conducted. Remarried couples identified nine areas of concern regarding former spouse interactions:

1. *The perpetuation of rapport.* Should former spouses be polite to each other, or be nonspeaking/hostile adversaries?

2. *Willingness to associate.* Under what circumstances should former spouses be willing to interact (e.g., lunch to discuss children, lunch for old times sake, hospital visits)?

3. *Former husband giving extra financial support.* Should a man give extra financial support to his ex-wife in exchange for more time with the children?

4. *Former wife giving extra time with children.* This issue is related to the concern in number 3.

5. *Former husband caring for children beyond the dictates of the legal decree.* Should the ex-husband be asked to take care of the children during times not outlined in the divorce agreement, and should he agree to do so if asked?

6. *Reciprocal influence in child-rearing behavior.* Should former spouses try to influence each other's parenting practices?

7. *Informing former husband of emergencies involving children.* Should an ex-wife inform her former spouse of medical emergencies involving the children?

8. *Discussing current marriage problems with former spouse.* Should marital problems related to the current marriage be discussed with a former spouse?

9. *Helping former husband with expenses.* Is it appropriate for an ex-wife to financially assist her ex-husband when he has the children (if he is paying her child support)?

These concerns were shared by individuals in remarried families in which the mothers had physical and legal custody of children and the fathers were legally mandated to provide child support. This list of concerns probably would differ if couples shared legal/physical custody or if children primarily resided with fathers.

Goetting assessed normative expectations by asking divorced and remarried adults to indicate what *should* be done in a series of hypothetical vignettes describing former spouses who were both remarried, relating to each other in situations reflecting the nine concerns described above. High consensus (arbitrarily defined as more than 75% agreement) was found on informing the former husband of emergencies, not discussing current marital problems, giving the former husband extra time with children for special occasions, and not helping the former husband with expenses. Low or moderate consensus was found on giving extra financial support in exchange for more time with children, willingness to associate with the ex-spouse, perpetuation of rapport beyond being polite in public, reciprocal influences in child-rearing behavior, and former husband caring for children beyond the legal requirements.

In a related study, Goetting (1980) again used vignettes to assess normative expectations about behavioral interactions between an individual's former spouse and current spouse. Less consensus was found on the behavioral expectations for this relationship than for relationships between former spouses. It was agreed generally that these relationships should be characterized by politeness in public settings and that information should be shared in the case of medical emergencies. Beyond these two areas, little consensus was achieved regarding how much these people should interact, nor was consensus found regarding what topics were appropriate for them to discuss. Few gender differences in normative beliefs were found in either study (Goetting, 1979, 1980).

Goetting was careful to point out that these investigations revealed nothing about the behaviors of people. She called for research that examines the changes in expectations and behaviors in former spouse relationships over time. A study by Anne-Marie Ambert (1989) did just that. Ambert found considerable agreement on norms regarding these relationships (e.g., they should be polite, ex-partners should work together for the sake of the children), but there was less agreement on the affective form these relationships should take (i.e., friendly, distant, or neutral). The actual behavior of the former spouses Ambert studied reflected the lack of agreement on the appropriate affect expected; she found great variability in the frequency of contact and the quality of former spouse relationships.

⁂ Grandparents

The role of grandparent is one of the most revered of all family roles. In fact, even the terms *grandmother* and *grandfather* evoke positive feelings (Ganong & Coleman, 1983). Cultural stereotypes portray grandparents as warm, caring individuals who are full of wisdom and love. In this idealized view, children can turn to grandparents when they need love, understanding, and kindly, helpful advice. In Western culture, grandparents stereotypically are seen as sources of support for grandchildren who may be experiencing stress accompanying their parents' divorce and remarriage.

Stereotypical views aside, the role of grandparents, always somewhat ambiguous, becomes even more so when their adult children divorce. After the divorce, grandparents become quasi-kin to their ex-daughter-in-law or ex-son-in-law (Bohannon, 1970). Normative expectations and prescriptions for quasi-kin interactions have yet to evolve. For example, how are grandparents now to relate to their ex-son-in-law or ex-daughter-in-law? The ambiguities of quasi-kin relationships introduce uncertainties regarding how intergenerational blood kin relationships should be conducted between grandparents and their grandchildren.

Although grandparents are quasi-kin of their former in-laws, they continue to be blood kin to their grandchildren. Nonetheless, the role that grandparents play with their grandchildren after divorce appears to depend on whether their child has custody of the grandchildren (Johnson, 1988). The large majority of grandparents in Johnson's study provided help such as financial assistance and some services to their children and grandchildren after divorce; however, maternal grandparents were more likely than the paternal grandparents to become involved in the life of their grandchildren. The postdivorce role of the paternal grandparents, whose son is usually the nonresidential parent, often is determined by the children's mother. Even when the involvement of the maternal and paternal grandparents immediately after divorce is similar, over time paternal grandparents have significantly less contact with grandchildren, and they provide less social and emotional support to their children and grandchildren (Johnson, 1988). In fact, the paternal grandparents may only see their grandchildren when the children are visiting their son.

There also are other gender differences in grandparent-grandchild contacts following divorce and remarriage. For example, few grandfathers remain actively involved with their divorced children and grandchildren independently of their wives. Johnson attributed this finding to the fact that women usually are the "kinkeepers" in families, the ones who decide about establishing and continuing relationships following family changes.

Ambert (1988) reported that the divorced people in her sample did not maintain positive relationships with quasi-kin (i.e., former parent-in-laws). In fact, deterioration of those relationships occurred very quickly. The reasons given were as follows:

> The former parents-in-law either stopped relating to them or were cold.
> The quasi-kin felt ill-at-ease with each other.
> The quasi-kin engaged in hostile behavior (e.g., yelling, accusing).

Some grandparents rejected not only their ex-in-law but also their grandchildren, although the only grandparents who did this were those who had other grandchildren.

Several scholars have speculated that intergenerational family ties are latent when families function well, but emerge as important relationships when families experience stress; maternal grandparents have been likened to "volunteer firefighters" (Cherlin & Furstenberg, 1986) and "watchdogs" (Troll, 1983) who come to the rescue when the family is disrupted but who otherwise remain in the background. Clingempeel, Colyar, Brand, and Hetherington (1992) labeled this tendency the "latent function hypothesis" and speculated that the stress of divorce would activate grandparents to become more involved in the lives of their divorcing child and grandchildren. Clingempeel and colleagues further speculated that the stress of a new remarriage might cause grandparents to remain involved with their child and grandchildren, at least temporarily. They found partial support for the latent function hypothesis in a longitudinal study of families and maternal grandparents: Divorce, but not remarriage, of custodial mothers was associated with higher grandparent-grandchild relationship involvement scores. The relationship between grandparents and their divorced daughter's children was of higher quality (i.e., more frequent contact and greater perceived closeness) than the relationship between grandparents and grandchildren in nuclear families or stepfather families. These results were corroborated over time by the perceptions of all three generations. The data did not support the hypothesis that there would be more involvement by maternal grandparents following their daughter's remarriage (Clingempeel et al., 1992). Cherlin and Furstenberg (1986), however, found that the remarriage of daughters did not alter the amount of contact between maternal grandparents and grandchildren, although the amount of financial assistance they provided was reduced when the daughter remarried.

Virtually all of the research on relationships between grandparents and grandchildren in remarried families has been conducted within the last decade. Clearly, much more research is needed. Given the potential source of support grandparents represent, it is imperative that more research be done to help us understand the nature of these relationships.

≈ Stepgrandparents

The relationship between stepgrandparents and stepgrandchildren is perhaps the least studied close relationship in remarried families. Like many other close relationships discussed in this book, normative expectations for relationships between stepgrandparents and stepchildren are unclear. In fact, normative expectations for this relationship are so ambiguous that some families may not even recognize the possibility of a relationship between the parents of a stepparent and the stepparent's stepchildren.

A number of factors probably affect the relationship between stepgrandparents and stepgrandchildren. For example, Cherlin and Furstenberg (1986) found that the older the children were when their parent remarried, the less likely they were to regard their stepgrandparents as of the same importance to them as their grandparents. Whether the stepgrandchild lives with the offspring of the stepgrandparent also may affect the relationship: Parents of residential stepparents may be more likely to have contact with their stepgrandchildren than parents of nonresidential stepparents. Another factor influencing the relationship is the acceptance of the remarriage by the stepgrandparents and stepgrandchildren (Sanders & Trygstad, 1989; Visher & Visher, 1979). If either the stepgrandparents or the stepgrandchildren are upset about or do not support the remarriage, it is less likely that a good relationship will develop between them.

Despite the lack of clarity surrounding the role of stepgrandparents, they can play an important part in the lives of their stepgrandchildren. Although Sanders and Trygstad found that children rated their grandparent as more involved than their stepgrandparent, 48% of stepgrandchildren viewed their relationship with their stepgrandparents as either important or extremely important, and 63% wanted more contact with their stepgrandparent. Stepgrandparents obviously were seen as a viable resource for a sizeable percentage of these stepgrandchildren.

In the relative dearth of research on the relationship between stepgrandparents and stepchildren, Henry, Ceglian, and Ostrander (1993) created a developmental model (see Table 5.2) that focuses on the transition to stepgrandparenthood. Although their model was designed to be useful to stepgrandparents seeking guidelines about how to proceed in establishing a relationship with their stepgrandchildren, it could serve also as a stimulus for further research on this relationship.

The four-stage model offers developmental tasks that provide excellent guidance to members of a generation less familiar with divorce and remarriage and probably less adept at handling the changes brought about by family transitions beyond their control. Stepgrandparents who can master these tasks can play an important role in the remarried family. According to Visher and Visher (1988), "Children are often more willing to accept a new set of grandparents than to accept a stepparent. Thus, if grandparents are willing to build bridges rather than walls, they can become constructive influences in the integrative process of the stepfamily" (p. 148).

Several of the relationships presented in this chapter are unusual in that they are not present in all families. For example, stepsiblings and stepgrandparents do not appear in first marriages or divorced families. The people in these various roles have the potential to be important influences on the stepchildren. For example, when things do not go well between the stepparent and the stepchild, the stepchild may need to turn to a trusted adult outside the household or may need to consult with a stepsibling

Table 5.2 The Developmental Stages and Tasks in the Transition to Stepgrandparenthood

Stage 1: Accepting the Losses

Developmental Tasks:
  Grieving and mourning the loss
  Letting go of the fantasy of "a lifelong happy marriage" between the adult-child and the adult-child's former spouse
  Accepting the loss of traditional grandparenthood
  Accepting fears about changing relationships with grandchildren
  Clarifying feelings about divorce and single parenting
  Dealing with one's feelings of anger, resentment, sadness, or failure

Stage 2: Accepting the Adult-Child's Single Status

Developmental Tasks:
  Adjusting to increased permeability of family boundaries
  Accepting reorganization of the adult-child's family
  Acknowledging the ambiguity in family roles
  Increasing contact with and support for adult-child without resuming parental roles
  Accepting ambiguity in grandparenting roles and seeking acceptable ways to maintain relationships with grandchildren
  Establishing a new relationship with the adult-child's former spouse
  Supporting the contact of grandchildren with the adult-child's former spouse
  Accepting the adult-child's new social network

Stage 3: Accepting the Adult-Child's Entrance Into a New Relationship

Developmental Tasks:
  Adapting to redefinition of the adult-child's family boundaries
  Acknowledging fears concerning the impact of a new relationship on all individuals involved
  Establishing open communication in new relationships to avoid pseudomutuality
  Placing the adult-child's former family into a historical perspective that allows grandchildren to have a sense of their roots and yet does not interfere with the acceptance of a new relationship
  Preparing to accept the potential of new family members in the adult-child's family system
  Acknowledging the existence of potential stepchildren and understanding their relationships with the adult-child's potential spouse
  Considering how potential new family members can be integrated into the extended family
  Providing a support system for grandchildren who fear their position in the new relationship or experience loyalty conflicts

(continued)

Table 5.2 Continued

Stage 4: Establishing New Relationships Within the Stepfamily Context

Developmental Tasks:
  Redefining family boundaries to include adult-child's new spouse and the stepchildren
  Developing realistic expectations for stepfamily living based on an understanding
    of the uniqueness of stepfamily structures
  Providing opportunities for developing bonds with the adult-child's new spouse
    and the stepgrandchildren
  Clarifying expectations for grandparenting and stepgrandparenting roles
  Restructuring family subsystems to accommodate expanding extended family
    systems
  Understanding differences in the legal relationships with grandchildren and
    stepgrandchildren
  Enhancing stepfamily integration through sharing information about family
    backgrounds and experiences with the adult-child's new spouse and the
    stepgrandchildren
  Establishing terminology to use when referring to persons in the complex of
    stepfamily relationships

to help make the behavior of a stepparent more understandable. These new roles and relationships have the potential to greatly enrich stepfamily living and need to be viewed in a more positive framework than has been typical in the past.

6

Clinical and
Developmental Perspectives

In Chapter 1 we mention the historical impact of clinical writers on the development of the study of remarried families. Their enormous influence is not only in the past, however; clinicians continue to play an important role in contributing to what is known about stepfamilies. In this chapter we (a) examine the predominant clinical perspectives on relationships in remarried families and (b) present some clinically inspired models of stepfamily development. We define *clinician* broadly as a helping professional working with families in a wide range of applied fields (e.g., family life educators, teachers, therapists).

A few years ago, in an integrative literature review, we compared the clinical and empirical literature on stepchildren and concluded that because there was little evidence of communication between researchers and clinicians, the two groups were segregated professionally (Ganong & Coleman, 1987). This scholarly division is unfortunate because researchers and clinicians have much to offer each other, and the body of knowledge about stepfamily relationships has taken longer to develop as a result of the limited exchange of information between the two groups. Moreover, as a result of this schism, the picture of stepfamily relationships drawn by either group of family professionals is necessarily incomplete and fragmented.

In the years since our review, a number of signs have indicated that the gap between stepfamily researchers and clinicians is narrowing. More researchers and clinicians are consulting each other's work (e.g., the ongoing, interdisciplinary Wingspread Conference on Remarried Families that meets alternately at NCFR and AAMFT meetings), and more research is being done by scholars who are also clinicians. It is in the interest of continuing this dialogue that we examine clinical work in this chapter.

❧ Clinical Perspectives

Family systems theories serve as the conceptual and theoretical framework for most stepfamily clinicians. Other theoretical perspectives sometimes are used by clinicians, particularly as the bases for interventions (e.g., cognitive behavioral theory, Gestalt), but even then, most clinicians conceptualize stepfamily relationships as occurring within the context of a system.

Aspects of family systems most often focused on by clinicians include rules governing patterns of interactions, roles, hierarchy, subsystems, boundaries, and emotional closeness (Ganong, Coleman, & Fine, in press). Of course, there are several schools of family systems thinking, and many of these are represented in the clinical literature on stepfamily relationships. What stepfamily clinicians tend to share in common, however, is the belief that stepfamily systems are quite different from nuclear families.

Stepfamily Characteristics

The first five chapters of this book contain numerous examples of how relationships in stepfamilies are different from those of first-marriage nuclear families. Most clinicians contend that understanding these differences is fundamental to understanding stepfamilies (cf. Martin, Martin, & Jeffers, 1993; Robinson, 1991; Sager et al., 1983; Visher & Visher, 1988). Clinicians maintain that even when stepfamilies appear structurally to be the same as nuclear families (e.g., the household contains two adults and children), they are different in several important ways.

Stepfamilies Are More Complex. As we note several times in this book, stepfamilies are generally more complex units than nuclear families. Stepfamilies are "fully formed" from the beginning. Unlike most first-marriage nuclear families, which typically begin as a married couple only, remarried families often begin with several relationships: the adult couple, stepparent-stepchild relationships, parent-child relationships, and possibly former-spouses, stepsiblings, siblings, and the nameless stepparent-bioparent relationships (remember "outlaws" from Chapter 1?). Remarriages after divorce may result in four adults in parental positions: a mother, a stepfather, a father, and a stepmother. Between the two households may be several sets of "his" and "hers" children, as well as the possibility of "ours" children if the remarried couple reproduces together. Both first-marriage nuclear families and stepfamilies have extended kin, but even here remarried families often have more people and more relationships (e.g., stepgrandparents in addition to grandparents). For adults and children to get their needs met in a newly formed stepfamily, it has been argued that stepfamilies have to integrate all of these relationships into some kind of workable whole (Visher & Visher, 1988), or what Goldner (1982) called a "new family culture."

More people and more relationships mean there must be clear communication between members in order for the system to function smoothly. Therefore, stepfamilies, by virtue of their complexity, place greater demands on their members' problem-solving and communication skills (Nelson & Levant, 1991).

The greater complexity of stepfamilies, it should be noted, does not imply that relationships in stepfamilies are inherently problematic and distressful. Although the tendency has been for our culture to assume that deviations from the nuclear family are bad, the additional complexity for stepfamilies may be an asset to some families and individuals and a deficit to others.

Clinicians postulate several reasons why greater complexity is an important contributor to the greater stress experienced by some stepfamily members. Some people simply lack the skills necessary to solve problems in complicated interpersonal environments (Clingempeel, Brand, & Segal, 1987; Fishman & Hamel, 1981). They may lack the cognitive complexity to deal with the sheer number and types of relationships that exist in a stepfamily, and so they become overwhelmed in trying to adapt to the multiplicity of relationships. As we discuss in Chapter 3, the majority of remarried couples do little to prepare themselves or their children for stepfamily life, and this lack of preparation may be especially damaging for those who have trouble handling complexity. This is more than an issue of intelligence, because some very bright people are not able to cope with multiple tasks at the same time.

Other individuals are not cognitively or emotionally comfortable dealing with ambiguity. Stepfamily relationships have many ambiguities, ranging from what stepparents should be called to how to celebrate holidays (Wald, 1981; Whiteside, 1989). A major source of ambiguity in remarried families concerns internal and external boundaries (Crosbie-Burnett, 1989b; McGoldrick & Carter, 1989; Minuchin, 1974; Pasley, 1987). *Internal boundaries* refer to rules about task performance and membership in specific subsystems within the stepfamily; *external boundaries* refer to rules about who is and is not a member of the stepfamily.

Individuals with low tolerance for ambiguity may push for decisions to be made too soon, they may avoid relationships in which they are not sure how to behave (e.g., stepparent-stepchild relationships), and they may rigidly insist on using a nuclear family model for stepfamily relationships even when it is inappropriate.

The use of a nuclear family model for stepfamily life is the major problem related to stepfamily complexity: A constant refrain heard from clinicians is that the nuclear family model is generally inappropriate for stepfamilies (cf. Fishman & Hamel, 1981; Goldner, 1982; Papernow, 1993; Sager et al., 1983; Visher & Visher, 1988). Stepfamilies use a nuclear family model when the expectation is that they will function as if they were a first-marriage family unit; that is, the residential stepparent is expected to replace the absent biological parent completely: emotionally, psychologically, financially, and behaviorally (e.g., disciplining children, making household rules). Children are to call the stepparent Mom or Dad, and steprelationships are expected to function as if they were biological relationships. In nuclear families, household membership and family membership usually are the same, so stepfamilies using this model try to establish boundaries around the household to exclude the nonresidential parent and his or her kin. Trying to establish boundaries means that efforts are made to discourage and even prohibit contact between nonresidential parents and their children and between grandparents and grandchildren (i.e., the parents of the absent parent). Even in postbereavement stepfamilies trying to emulate nuclear families, children are encouraged to think of the stepparent as their new parent, as household boundaries are drawn psychologically as well as physically. In some stepfather families, stepchildren begin using the last name of the stepfather so that they will be seen by others as a nuclear family, and adoption may be initiated by some stepfamilies in efforts to legally complete the ideological and behavioral metamorphosis from a stepfamily into a nuclear family. *The Brady Bunch*, the famous television stepfamily, is an example of a family using the nuclear family model.

If the nuclear family model worked for the television Brady family, why do clinicians consider this particular response to complexity to be a problem for most stepfamilies? First, to function and assume the identity of a nuclear family, stepfamilies must engage in massive denial and distortion of reality (Goldner, 1982). This deceit takes enormous emotional energy and has considerable costs psychologically and interpersonally. It is as if stepfamily members are asked to wipe the slate clean, to forget about prior relationships, and to begin as if nothing that went on before the remarriage actually happened. Second, former spouses and their families must be cut off from children, resulting in emotional losses for adults and children alike. Feelings of abandonment, anger, guilt, resentment, and unresolved feelings of loss are likely when ties between nonresidential parents and children are severed.

Sometimes a remarried parent who severs the ties between his or her children and former spouse finds that these actions have the opposite effect: Children harbor resentments toward the residential parent and stepparent and fantasize about the "perfect" parent with whom they have no contact. Rather than emotionally replace the parent with the stepparent, these children may never accept the stepparent whose presence has robbed them of knowing their biological parent.

Third, it is unrealistic to expect that all members of a stepfamily will accept this model for their family relationships. If all members do not agree to function as a nuclear family, then this leads to stressful interactions with the dissenters. For example, if a nonresidential parent refuses to be replaced by the stepparent, then he or she may institute a legal custody battle over the children. Or if a child refuses to accept a stepparent as a parent, then the stepparent may feel hurt and may withdraw emotionally from the child.

Not only is it unrealistic to expect everyone to agree, but it also is unrealistic to expect relationships to be similar to the biological relationships found in nuclear families (Mills, 1984; Visher & Visher, 1978). Leslie and Epstein (1988) pointed out that expecting the newly remarried couple to coparent smoothly is expecting them "to work like a team even though they have had no practice" (p. 154), an analogy that could be applied to other relationships in remarried families as well.

Goldner (1982) called the use of the nuclear family model "the retreat from complexity" (p. 205). Stepfamilies, lacking established rituals and rules for behaving, try to re-create the nuclear family because it is what they know and because it is simpler to deal with than the reality of stepfamily complexity and ambiguity. One reason why families in general may run into difficulties is that people have trouble thinking creatively about different ways to be a family (Minuchin & Nichols, 1993); if this is so for families in general, then the inability to act and to think flexibly about how to "do" family life may be especially relevant for stepfamilies (Fishman & Hamel, 1981).

Despite the prevailing clinical perspective on this issue, it is possible that acting like and thinking of themselves as a nuclear family unit may work for some stepfamilies. It is probable that some stepfamilies do function as if they were a nuclear family without encountering problems that would send them to a clinician for help. We hypothesize that the nuclear family ideology may be effective when (a) the nonresidential parent and his or her kin have no contact with children in the remarried family household, (b) the children are young at the time of remarriage, so they do not remember much, if anything, about prior family life, and (c) all stepfamily members want to recreate the nuclear family and agree, implicitly or explicitly, to do so. These hypotheses have yet to be tested. In fact, no researcher has examined the relation between functioning as a nuclear family and the quality of stepfamily relationships.

Children Often Are Members of Two Households. Another difference between nuclear family systems and stepfamily systems is that stepchildren may hold membership in two households. Of course, many stepchildren have virtually no contact with a nonresidential parent (Furstenberg & Nord, 1985), but the increased prevalence of joint legal and physical custody in recent years may result in more stepchildren being part-time members of two households in the future. For those who do hold membership in two households, the arrangements can range from almost full-time residence in one household with rare visits to the other household, to half-time residence in both. Most stepchildren who belong to two households probably fall between these two extremes, residing mostly with one parent but spending some time periodically with the other parent.

When children are members of two households, it means those households are gaining and losing children from time to time. For example, Jack and Jill, a remarried couple, raise Jill's child from a prior marriage during the week. On alternate weekends, they either add Jack's three children from a prior relationship, or they have no children in the household because Jill's child is with the father and Jack's children are with their mother.

This *accordion effect* creates logistical and emotional complications for adults and children. Children who go back and forth may have difficulty adjusting to different sets of rules and expectations (Visher & Visher, 1982). Standards for behavior may differ markedly between the two households. Children usually can adjust to differing expectations, especially if both sets of adults assist them, but differing rules for children also can be a rallying point for conflict between former spouses. Discipline issues may be accentuated when children belong to two households (Pill, 1981; Visher & Visher, 1978). Stepparents may have a difficult time deciding how to make children behave who are only in the residence part of the time. Should they be held to the same rules and expectations for behavior as children who are full-time residents of the household? Biological parents are sometimes reluctant to discipline children they see only occasionally, wanting instead to accentuate pleasurable interactions with the children.

Adults, too, must make adjustments when children are part of two households. The entrances and exits of children into a household take tolls of time and physical and emotional energy. The frequently changing numbers of people in the household may be stressful to some stepfamily members, whereas others thrive on the excitement of the constant changes. Communication with the former spouse becomes a necessity when children are shared, and this may be a difficult and challenging task for fiery foes (Ahrons & Rodgers, 1987).

Sharing children also introduces issues related to control and power. In first-marriage families, parents have sole responsibility for financial decisions regarding children, they have all legal rights and responsibilities for their children, they can make the strongest claim on their children's love and affection, and they have the sole authority to make decisions related to child rearing. In contrast, stepfamilies in which children belong to two households must share, to some degree, the financial, legal, emotional, and child-rearing rights and responsibilities for the children (Coale Lewis, 1985; Walker & Messinger, 1979). This sharing could, conceivably, be a positive aspect of remarried families: When child-rearing responsibilities are shared, fewer demands are put on any one person or household. However, parents and stepparents often feel uncomfortable over not having sole control. The imitation of nuclear families may be an attempt by some stepfamilies to gain a sense of control. The danger is that stepfamily households may try to close boundaries around their household (exclude the other household) as a means of gaining a sense of control (Coale Lewis, 1985). Attempts to exclude the other household lead to greater conflict between former spouses, and loyalty conflicts for children, who are put into the position of choosing one parent over the other. Loyalty conflicts for children are believed to be extremely common, even among stepchildren who have good relationships with all of the parents and stepparents (Lutz, 1983; Sager, Walker, Brown, Crohn, & Rodstein, 1981).

Sometimes a parent will try to enlist his or her children in a campaign against the other parent. This tactic may be done to punish the former spouse, but it is also done to gain control over one's household by turning the child against the other parent. Paradoxically, this strategy not only can damage the relationship with one parent but also can hinder the development of satisfying relationships with all of the adults in the remarried family. This is so because children who are put in the position of being asked to side with a parent have increased power in the stepfamily, sometimes more than any of the parents or stepparents. For example, a child with warring parents can threaten to go live with the other parent if household rules are not to his or her liking. These children can, in essence, peddle their affection and their presence to the highest bidder. It is too much for most children to handle, and although they may seek power, they often are relieved when such control over the important adults in their lives is removed. Such power and control generally are unheard of in first-marriage families.

Biological Parents Elsewhere in Actuality or in Memory. Children do not have to go back and forth physically between households, children and nonresidential parents do not have to have contact with each other, and, in fact, parents do not have to be living, for the nonresidential biological parent to be an important factor in stepfamily relationships (Visher & Visher, 1988). If children are old enough to remember life with their deceased or absent parent, then that parent could be a significant figure to them. Even when children do not remember living with the absent parent, stories told to them by grandparents, older siblings, the remaining parent, other family members, and friends help create a memory of the absent parent for the children.

Parents with whom they have not had much contact sometimes take on a larger-than-life status for children. In short, children imagine a perfect parent and, with no conflicting real-life evidence to the contrary, can cling tenaciously to the belief that their lives would be better if they lived with their "real" parent instead of the flawed parent and a stepparent. Stepparents and parents in daily interaction with a child cannot compare favorably in the child's mind to an idealized absent parent who would treat the child exactly as he or she wants to be treated. Having to compete with an idealized absent parent contributes to a feeling of hopelessness on the part of stepparents and parents (Visher & Visher, 1988).

Stepfamily Members Have Different Family Histories. Another unique characteristic of stepfamilies is that the members have different family histories. Adults in nuclear families enter marriage with individual family-of-origin histories, but they go on to develop a mutual family culture with its own rituals and history. Children raised in nuclear families share that history and common family culture. Consequently in nuclear families there is a shared past and expectations for a common future. Moreover, in nuclear families the shared history contributes to a sense of family bonds and the creation of a family identity that feels normal and right to family members (Goldner, 1982).

Remarried families, lacking this shared history as a unit, not only have to figure out new patterns of interacting but must do so while struggling to develop a common sense of family, a common identity (Ahrons & Perlmutter, 1982; Goldner, 1982; Pill, 1990). The absence of family rituals and shared rules for conduct, two dimensions of family life that frequently go unnoticed in nuclear families because they can be taken for granted, create a feeling of artificiality for stepfamilies (Imber-Black & Roberts, 1993; Whiteside, 1988). In stepfamilies a parent and child(ren) have mutual experiences and shared recollections of a family life that does not include the stepparent (and any children he or she may have). This is important, not only because some stepfamily members are excluded from "remember when . . ." stories, but also because different relationship histories can result in patterns of living and relating that seem odd to those who were not involved in developing those patterns (Wald, 1981). This joining of family cultures may cause confusion in the period of transition after remarriage and, if not resolved, may result in a chronic sense that things do not feel right or natural in the stepfamily (Goldner, 1982). Unless a premium is put on communicating expectations clearly and being flexible in adapting these different ways of being a family, misunderstandings and mistaken assumptions will occur.

Parent-Child Bonds Are Older Than Spousal Bonds. Another major characteristic that distinguishes stepfamilies from nuclear families is that the parent-child bond is formed prior to the marital bond. This timing may mean, in addition to the shared history differences mentioned above, that the primary emotional tie for newly remarried parents is with their children, rather than with their new spouse. Unlike first-time marriages, couples in stepfamilies must develop a cohesive marital unit at the same time they are maintaining parent-child relationships and beginning stepparent-child ties. At least in the early periods of stepfamily life, it is not unreasonable to assume that the parents' primary loyalty will be to their child. In remarriages involving children, the couple lack the luxury of months and years alone to adjust to each other, as is typical in first marriages. As a result, bonds may be somewhat tenuous and fragile.

Fishman and Hamel (1981) called the parent-child bond predating the couple bonds in remarried families an "anomalous family life course pattern" (p. 186) because stepfamilies are at a later point in the family life course (parent-child relationships) and at an earlier point in the marital career. The parent-child relationship, having been together longer, is in a better position to shape the family culture than is the marital relationship: thus the anomaly.

The tasks for stepfamilies are to (a) establish a strong marital relationship, (b) clarify the boundaries around the marital dyad (Coale Lewis, 1985), and (c) assist the stepparent in finding ways to relate to the stepchild (Cissna et al., 1990). Stepfamilies find themselves with subsystems that have competing needs (Papernow, 1987; Visher & Visher, 1991). For example, in this case parent-child dyads and spousal dyads may compete for the time and attention of the biological parent/marital partner. Parents may find themselves feeling tugged and experiencing loyalty conflicts between their children and their new partners.

Individual, Marital, and Family Life Cycles Are More Likely to Be Incongruent. That parent-child relationships predate the marital relationship is but one example of incongruencies in life cycles. Another discrepancy is the greater age difference between partners in remarried couples than in first-marriage couples. Remarried couples who are vastly different in age may have children who are vastly different in ages, creating several developmental incongruencies. For example, Ward, a man in his 50s whose children are in their 20s and 30s, remarried June, a woman in her mid-30s whose children are preschoolers. Ward and June's *remarried family* is functioning at two stages of the family life cycle at once (Goldner, 1982), while the *marriage* is at a beginning (newlywed) stage. The individuals are also out of sync with family demands and with each other: Ward may be feeling the need to relax and to slow down, taking time to enjoy the fruits of his earlier labors, whereas June may be feeling the need to work harder in her career so that she can solidify her standing with her employer. Ward, who may have thought his PTA days were long past, now can contemplate over a decade more of "back-to-school" nights. June, who may not have thought much about grandmotherhood, could instantly become a stepgrandmother to children the age of her preschoolers. One of the wackiest examples of developmental incongruencies in remarried families is the recent case of Rolling Stones' guitarist Bill Wyman's son. This young man married the mother of his father's ex-wife (young Wyman's former stepmother), making Bill Wyman's former mother-in-law his new daughter-in-law, and young Wyman's former stepmother his new stepdaughter!

Other, less exotic incongruencies occur fairly frequently. For instance, a newly remarried couple may encourage the development of family closeness by planning family outings and activities at the same time that an adolescent stepchild is moving away from family members and toward personal independence. This is an example of marital/family developmental needs being at odds with developmental needs of individuals in the family. Intraindividual discrepancies also can occur: Stepparents who have never had children begin, simultaneously, a marital and a child-rearing career. Developmental discrepancies put demands on the individuals involved to confront multiple developmental tasks, for some of which they have had no psychological, social, or behavioral preparation (McGoldrick & Carter, 1989). Dealing with issues that are chronologically nonnormative is more stressful. When these discrepancies occur in stepfamilies, it may be difficult for the family to feel normal and natural to the participants.

Stepfamilies Begin After Many Losses and Changes. As we discuss in Chapter 2, remarried families generally are formed after several family transitions. Each transition represents multiple changes for stepfamily members, such as changes in relationships, role expectations, self-identity, and family identity. Some of these changes entail losses that must be mourned. There are lost opportunities, lost dreams, losses in relationships, and losses in experiences. If losses from prior family situations are not mourned before stepfamilies are formed, and if successful adaptation to previous changes have not been made, then "the stepfamily inherits trouble" (Coale Lewis, 1985, p. 16). The view of many clinicians is that energies cannot be focused on stepfamily relationships until earlier issues and developmental tasks are resolved (Sager et al., 1981; Visher & Visher, 1982, 1988, 1991). For example, if a single mother has not established patterns of disciplining and controlling her children before she remarries, then there will be problems if the stepfather tries to impose rules and restrictions on them.

Children and Adults Come With Expectations From Previous Families. Expectations from previous family life experiences are not inherently good or bad. Clinicians focus on the unrealistic expectations that contribute to problematic interactions in remarried families (Kaplan & Hennon, 1992; Leslie & Epstein, 1988; McGoldrick & Carter, 1989; Pill, 1990). We already have discussed one of the most troublesome unrealistic expectations—the expectation that stepfamilies will function just like nuclear families.

Other unrealistic expectations also have been identified. Some remarried adults assume that relationships in remarried families will be good without any effort. The prime example of this assumption is the "myth of instant love" (see Chapter 4), in which stepparents are expected to feel love and affection instantly for their stepchildren. This expectation causes stepparents who do not experience instantaneous love feelings to feel guilty, to deny their ambivalent feelings, and to push too hard for a relationship with the stepchild, rather than to let a bond with the child develop gradually and at the child's pace.

Adults also sometimes expect that discipline from the stepparent will be accepted by stepchildren without question and that new family traditions and rituals will evolve magically without planning and effort. When these unrealistic expectations fail to materialize, remarried adults may feel confused and anxious and eventually dissatisfied.

Adults who remarry after a previous relationship that was unhappy may hold expectations that are not unrealistically high but that are unrealistic in other ways. For example, remarriers whose prior marriage ended in divorce may so desperately want the remarriage to last that they will adhere to myths such as "Keep criticism to oneself and focus on the positive" and "If things are not going well, focus on what went wrong in the past and make sure it does not happen again" (Coleman & Ganong, 1985). Expectations such as these discourage open communication and lead to the denial of problems and what family therapists call "pseudomutuality" (McGoldrick & Carter, 1989). *Pseudomutuality* within remarried families is defined as the tendency to deny history, ambivalence, and conflict (Sager et al., 1983). Rather than confront and challenge each other when things are not going smoothly, family members who expect the remarriage to fail "walk on eggs." Problems do not get resolved, thus leading to feelings of alienation and powerlessness.

The complexity of stepfamilies contributes to problems as a result of differing expectations. In first-marriage families the couple brings expectations to marriage that are based partly on observations and experiences in their families of origin and partly on cultural expectations regarding marriage. Later, as they become parents, they again draw on personal experiences they had while growing up and cultural expectations to guide their behaviors in the roles of parents. In remarried families, adults bring expectations based not only on family experiences observed while growing up but also on adult experiences in prior marital/parental/family situations. Children also bring expectations, as do former spouses and extended kin. To this mix are added cultural expectations regarding remarriage and stepparenting. There are sometimes many competing agendas and beliefs in remarried families (Leslie & Epstein, 1988; Visher & Visher, 1991).

Stepfamilies Are Less Supported by the Society as a Whole. Clinicians generally subscribe to Cherlin's hypotheses related to the lack of institutionalized societal supports for remarried families. In their face-to-face work with stepfamily members, clinicians observe circumstances that might be thought of as microsystem operationalizations of the macrosystem level of custom, language, and law that Cherlin (1978) wrote about.

For example, stepparents who are involved in their stepchildren's schooling frequently find that the customs of school systems are such that little allowance is made for the presence of stepparents. Enrollment forms may have places for parents' names only, seniors are given only two tickets for their parents to attend graduation ceremonies, and teachers are ill-prepared for a child to have three or more parents/stepparents show up on "back to school" night (Coleman, Ganong, & Henry, 1984b). Other social organizations, such as youth groups, religious groups, and health care systems, are based on policies and procedures designed primarily for nuclear families (Coleman, Ganong, & Henry, 1984a; Ganong, 1993). Stepfamilies and other family forms are usually welcome to participate in these organizations, but few attempts, if any, are made to accommodate organizational practices to facilitate stepfamily participation. This sort of subtle social pressure on stepfamilies to act like nuclear families if they want to be accepted puts undue pressure on relationships within remarried families to imitate as closely as possible nuclear family relationships. Paradoxically, rather than provide buffers for stress, the customs of social systems that interact with stepfamilies sometimes increase the stress on stepfamily relationships.

There is also less informal social support for stepfamily relationships. As we discuss in Chapter 3, stepfamilies, in an effort to avoid stigma, often do not let outsiders know of their stepfamily status. Although this concealment may be an effective strategy to avoid unpleasant reactions from others, it unfortunately excludes others from providing assistance, encouragement, and moral support. In hiding their step status to avoid stigma, members of remarried families may be contributing unintentionally to their social isolation (Pill, 1981).

Daily encounters with language that seems to invalidate their family status also is seen as a factor in adding to stepfamily stress. The prefix *step* triggers negative reactions and may be a pejorative (Fine, 1986; Ganong & Coleman, 1983; Ganong, Coleman, & Kennedy, 1990). The term *stepchild* is used metaphorically to refer to someone or something that is abused, neglected, or unwanted (Coleman & Ganong, 1987a). The proliferation of labels for remarried families (see Chapter 1) may be less a matter of social scientists being unable to agree on a suitable term than a consequence of the cultural ambivalence experienced toward steprelationships and remarriage. Because group labels influence thoughts and feelings about the group, attempts have been made to relabel stepfamilies.

Other language usage, such as describing biological parents as real or natural parents, implicitly conveys the message that stepparents (and adoptive parents, foster parents, etc.) are unreal or unnatural. Identifying nuclear families as normal, real, or traditional similarly signifies that other families are abnormal, unreal, and nontraditional. The use of language can serve to legitimize certain family forms and to place others on the fringe of acceptability. Language helps shape thinking, and language about relationships in remarried families may make it more difficult for family members to develop positive identities and satisfying relationships (Coleman & Ganong, 1987a). Family laws also may be seen as failing to provide support to remarried families.

Legal Relationships Between Stepparent and Stepchild Are Ambiguous or Nonexistent. Stepparents generally have been overlooked in federal and state laws in the United States; they have few legal responsibilities toward their stepchildren, and few rights as well (Chambers, 1990; Fine & Fine, 1992; Ramsey, 1986). Changes in family law in recent years indirectly impact the legal relation between stepparents and stepchildren (e.g., more states are allowing third-party requests for postdivorce custody), but there is little consensus on what legal changes are needed and little political pressure on legislatures to alter existing policies and laws (Chambers, 1990). The American Bar Association has established a Standing Committee on the Rights and Responsibilities of Stepparents that has drafted a model act (Tenenbaum, 1991), but there is relatively little impetus to push for rapid legal changes.

Clinicians contend that the absence of a legal relationship serves as a barrier to the development of emotionally close stepparent-stepchild bonds. Unlike biological parents, whose obligations to their children are dictated in state and federal statutes, stepparents' obligations to stepchildren are based on whatever family members want them to be. Although this flexibility could be seen as an advantage, it is likely that for many stepparents, the absence of legal ties just further adds to the ambiguity and lack of control they feel. Chambers (1990) contended that the legal (non)status of stepparents has little pragmatic impact on stepparents and stepchildren, but as of yet no researchers have investigated this.

Stepfamily Systems Are Not as Emotionally Close. Stepfamilies are not as close as nuclear families (Kennedy, 1985; Peek, Bell, Waldron, & Sorell, 1988; Pill, 1990; Pink & Wampler, 1985), and stepparent-child dyads are not as emotionally close as parent-child dyads (Anderson & White, 1986; Ganong & Coleman, 1986; Hetherington & Clingempeel, 1992; Hobart, 1989). Although not all researchers have found more closeness among biological relationships (T. Smith, 1991), these are fairly robust findings; consistent results have been found by researchers who have used several methods with varying samples to assess emotional closeness.

What meaning to assign to attenuated closeness in stepfamilies is not clear. For example, how much of an issue should closeness be in stepfamilies? Should stepfamilies and steprelationships be as close as nuclear families and blood kin relationships? Is it possible for well-functioning stepfamilies to have optimal levels of closeness that differ from those of nuclear families? Research using standardized instruments on nonclinical samples of stepfamilies found that although stepfamilies were not as close as nuclear families, they were well within the functional range on these instruments, a finding suggesting that patterns of effective stepfamily functioning may differ from those of nuclear families (Anderson & White, 1986; Coleman & Ganong, 1987a; Orleans, Palisi, & Caddell, 1989). However, not all studies have found that stepfamilies have different patterns of interactions from nuclear families (Peek, Bell, Waldren, & Sorell, 1988; Waldren, Bell, Peek, & Sorell, 1990). This is an area that needs to be investigated much more fully.

Do stepfamilies become closer over time? One implicit assumption held by many family clinicians and researchers is that functional stepfamilies become closer over time until they are nearly indistinguishable from nuclear families in emotional closeness and patterns of functioning. The few longitudinal studies that have been conducted on stepfamilies offer little empirical support for this speculation (Ganong & Coleman, in press; Hetherington & Clingempeel, 1992; Kurdek, 1991b).

We noted earlier in this book that stepfamilies are sometimes called *blended* or *reconstituted* families. An implicit expectation of both of those labels is that stepfamilies will be as close as first-marriage families. Remarried adults are frequently guilty of expecting more cohesion and closeness than children find comfortable (McGoldrick & Carter, 1989; Papernow, 1993). This push for cohesion stresses children (Kompara, 1980) and can result either in pseudomutuality or rebellion and withdrawal by children (Sager et al., 1983). An unintended result of this adult push for cohesion is that stepfamilies become less, rather than more, cohesive because children actively pull away (McGoldrick & Carter, 1989; Visher & Visher, 1988).

Other Clinically Identified Problems in Stepfamily Relationships

In addition to the relationship difficulties associated with the stepfamily characteristics just discussed, clinicians have identified several other problems experienced by members of remarried families. In Table 6.1 is a list of issues and problems found in clinical works on stepchildren and their relationships (Ganong &

Coleman, 1987). Nearly all of these problems have been mentioned briefly or discussed earlier in this book, either in this chapter or in the first five chapters. Unfortunately a thorough examination of each of these concerns is beyond the scope and purpose of this book, but we do want to focus for a moment on an area of clinical interest in remarried family relationships that also has received attention by researchers in recent years, cognitive factors related to stepfamily relationships.

Belief Systems/Cognitive Factors. Clinicians and researchers interested in remarried families have long believed that relationships were influenced by what we call "cognitive factors or belief systems" (i.e., thoughts, expectations, myths, cognitive schemas, and beliefs). From the early researchers who wrote about the stigma associated with stepparenthood (W. Smith, 1953) and the problems with stepfamily labels (Bernard, 1956), to the early clinicians who wrote about stepparents having difficulty defining their roles (Fast & Cain, 1966), cognitive factors have been seen as important elements in shaping the development of stepfamily relationships.

Clinicians argue that stepfamilies are prone to belief system problems because most of the cultural beliefs about how families should be are based on nuclear families (Coale Lewis, 1985; Visher & Visher, 1988). Thus these beliefs do not provide members of remarried families much assistance in anticipating problems and figuring out workable solutions to existing problems. Cultural beliefs about remarried families tend to be unhelpful as well because they are almost always either negative (e.g., stepparents are mean and wicked) or incredibly unrealistic (e.g., stepparents will love their stepchildren as much as they do their biological children, children should be loyal to one mother and one father only) (Coale Lewis, 1985; Coleman & Ganong, 1987a; Ganong, Coleman, & Mapes, 1990; Leslie & Epstein, 1988; Visher & Visher, 1988). Cultural belief systems are not the only cognitive factors affecting relationships in remarried families, however.

Individuals also hold idiosyncratic beliefs about family relationships (Fine & Schwebel, 1991). For example, a stepmother who has not had children of her own may believe that children *must always obey* her or else it means they do not respect her. Other

Table 6.1 Issues and Problems Found in Clinical Works on Stepchildren

Family Dynamics	Lifestyle difference
Loyalty	Holidays
Coparental conflicts	Birth order changes
Biological parent-child bonds	Lack of privacy
Jealousy	Increased activity
Custody	Time between marriages
Sibling relationships	
Couple relations	*Incomplete Institution*
Idealization of absent parent	Role confusion
Pseudomutuality	No legal ties
Scapegoating	No societal rituals
Child born of remarried parents	Family identity confusion
Sexually charged atmosphere	Kinship terms
Push for cohesion	How much to parent
Surnames	No model for stepparent-child
Turf or space issues	relations
Two households	How much affection to show
Boundary issues	How to show affection
Triangulation	Money issues
Rejection by stepparents	
Extreme intimacy	*Emotional Responses*
Discipline	Guilt
Competition and rivalry	Loss, mourning
Grandparents	Feeling unwanted
Stepchild expelled	Reuniting fantasies
Subgroups within family	Ambivalence
Rejection of stepparent	Feeling responsible for parent's
Low cohesion	loneliness
Poor communication	Stress, emotions, or greater
Exclusion of parental child	vulnerability
Scapegoating noncustodial parent	Identity confusion
Stepmothers who lack experience	Fear of being misunderstood
Stepsibling relations	Anger
	Fear of family breakup
Transitional Adjustments	Rebellion
Adjustment to change	
Conflict in merging	*Stepfamily Expectations*
Myth of instant love	Negative image
No shared rules	Love conquers all
Lack of shared rituals	Step same as nuclear
Child not told prior to marriage	Stepparent as rescuer
No shared history	Higher expectations
Age at parental remarriage	

NOTE: Data from "Effects of Parental Remarriage on Children: An Updated Comparison of Theories, Methods, and Findings From Clinical and Empirical Research" by L. Ganong & M. Coleman, 1987, *Remarriage and Stepparenting Today: Current Research and Theory*, K. Pasley & M. Ihinger-Tallman (Eds.), pp. 130-131.

idiosyncratic beliefs may be more general, constituting what might be considered personal rules for living and relating. When these individually held beliefs are irrational or illogical, such as when a person thinks that other people *must always be fair* to him or her or when an individual thinks *he or she must always be perfect*, then emotional reactions and behaviors toward others are likely to be impacted negatively (Ellis & Grieger, 1977).

Distorted *perceptions* of other family members, dysfunctional *attributions* of why other people behave as they do, and inaccurate *expectancies* or predictions of how another person will behave in the future are other cognitive factors that have been hypothesized to influence stepfamily relationships (Fine & Schwebel, 1991; Kurdek, 1991a, 1991b; Kurdek & Fine, 1991, 1993; Leslie & Epstein, 1988). Given the relative absence of clear cultural definitions related to stepfamily roles, the intensity of feelings and values related to family life, in general, and the need for humans to make sense of the world in which they live, it seems probable that the relation between cognitive factors and relationship adjustment will receive increasing attention from both clinicians and researchers.

໒ Stepfamily Development

The processes of development in a stepfamily system are different from those in a nuclear family system. Several writers have identified the developmental tasks and stages experienced by stepfamilies (e.g., McGoldrick & Carter, 1989; Papernow, 1984, 1993; Ransom, Schlesinger, & Derdeyn, 1979; Rodgers & Conrad, 1986). Most of these attempts have focused primarily on the developmental dynamics of the stepfamily *household;* dynamics related to the *binuclear system* and *extended family networks* have received relatively less attention.

໒ Models of Stepfamily Development

A number of models of stepfamily development have been proposed. We briefly examine three of these models, all of which are based, at least in part, on family systems concepts.

Mills's Model for Stepfamily Development

Mills's clinically derived model is less a description of how stepfamilies *actually* develop than it is a proposal for how they *could* develop in a flexible, functional manner (Mills, 1984). Mills outlined what he saw as requirements for any developmental model of stepfamilies. Although this list of criteria was designed for clinically useful models, most of them can apply equally well to empirical models:

- It should not be identified as the only way that a stepfamily can develop, but as one of several functional approaches that a stepfamily might follow.
- It must allow for the simultaneous achievement of a number of different, and sometimes competing, developmental tasks of individual family members and the stepfamily as a whole.
- It must take into account the fact that parent-child bonds are older and more enduring than stepparent-child bonds.
- It must be aware of the binuclear nature of many stepfamilies, even in situations where the nonresidential parent is not physically available.
- It should be useful not only during the formative period but also in later periods of stepfamily life.

Mills's model is based on his clinical observation that many stepfamilies create problems for themselves by trying to re-create a nuclear family pattern of interaction. In particular, problems ensue when attempts are made to base the stepparent-stepchild relationship on a parent-child model, a goal that Mills (1984) defined explicitly as inappropriate. The model emphasizes the necessity for the marital pair to assume executive control of the family, to plan what kind of role the stepparent(s) will play, as well as to decide the type of structure to establish within the family that will help individual family members get their needs met. These plans are based on previously decided goals for the stepfamily. The idea is to place most of the responsibility for decision making on the subsystem that presumably has the greatest motivation to make the family a success—the adults who decided to marry. The focus of the majority of decisions is on the stepparent-stepchild relationship, the subsystem that may be the most important in predicting stepfamily satisfaction (Crosbie-Burnett, 1984).

Stepfamilies are encouraged to be creative in choosing roles and rules that work for the specific needs of the family members. For example, families can consider drawing on ideas related to a variety of roles (e.g., coach, sister or brother, friend, aunt or uncle, advisor, parent) when deciding on the stepparents' roles. Some families could even decide that the stepparent would assume different roles for different stepchildren, on the basis of the stepchildren's expressed needs, ages, or gender.

Biological parents are put in control of limit setting for children, reducing the opportunity for conflicts between stepchildren and stepparents and eliminating triangling dynamics between parent, stepparent, and the child. Stepparents are given the task of bonding emotionally with stepchildren by engaging in fun and nurturing interactions. Household rules are established, with an eye toward building a set of rituals and traditions for the stepfamily.

The recommendations in this model are thought-provoking and could be subjected to empirical study, albeit with some difficulty. To date, little interest has been shown by researchers in testing some of the propositions that could be derived from Mills's developmental model.

McGoldrick and Carter's Developmental Phase Model

McGoldrick and Carter's model, based partly on an earlier clinically inspired model (Ransom et al., 1979), consists of three phases or steps, each of which is accompanied by "prerequisite attitudes" and "developmental issues" that must be addressed. The first two phases are premarriage periods, reflecting McGoldrick and Carter's (1989) emphasis on the necessity for a couple and their children to plan ahead for remarriage. The *prerequisite attitudes* are emotional tasks that must be resolved before individuals and families can work on the accompanying "developmental issues." An example of a prerequisite attitude is, "Final resolution of attachment to previous spouse and the ideal of 'intact' family," which must be resolved before such developmental issues as "restructuring family boundaries to allow for inclusion of new spouse-stepparent" are addressed successfully.

McGoldrick and Carter's model emphasizes resolving issues related to the prior marriage and divorce before remarriage and step-family issues are confronted. Tasks are outlined for individuals, family subsystems, the binuclear family unit, and the extended family system. The goal for stepfamilies to work toward, according to this model, is to have an open system with workable boundaries.

McGoldrick and Carter identified several predictors of difficulty in making the transition to remarriage:

- a wide discrepancy in the life cycle stages of "his" family and "her" family
- denial of earlier losses and a short time period between marriages
- unresolved, intense feelings for the former spouse
- expecting that the children will easily accept a stepparent, and a general lack of understanding children's emotional reactions to remarriage
- inability to give up the ideal of the nuclear family
- efforts to draw firm boundaries around the stepfamily household and pushing for cohesion too quickly
- trying to exclude the nonresidential biological parents and grandparents
- denying difficulties
- a shift in physical custody near the time of remarriage

These speculations, based on Carter and McGoldrick's clinical experiences, have not stimulated much empirical work even though they first were proposed more than a decade ago.

The Stepfamily Cycle

A model drawn from Gestalt psychology and family systems theories identifies seven stages of stepfamily development: (a) fantasy, (b) immersion, (c) awareness, (d) mobilization, (e) action, (f) contact, and (g) resolution (Papernow, 1993). This model blends individual and family dynamics together to describe the developmental processes of stepfamilies. It is based on both Papernow's experiences as a clinician and a qualitative study of both clinical and nonclinical stepfamilies (Papernow, 1984, 1987, 1993).

The first three stages of fantasy, immersion, and awareness are considered to be the *early stages*. The developmental tasks of the early stages include giving up comforting fantasies, working through confusion and disappointment when fantasies are not met, and identifying and communicating about different experiences related to different positions in the remarried family. There is a wide variation in the amount of time it takes a stepfamily to complete the early stages. *Middle stages* include mobilization and action. In these stages the stepfamily gets to work at becoming a stepfamily unit; conflict is aired during mobilization and is resolved during the action stage. In the two *later stages*, contact and resolution, the family can function without consciously being aware of stepfamily issues.

Fantasy. Stepfamily members bring a host of fantasies, wishes, and unrealistic expectations to the beginning of the stepfamily. Some of these are based on previous family experiences, some are due to a lack of information about remarried families, and some are based on cultural ideals and belief systems, but the goals seem to be to ease the pain of prior losses. Adults often wish for the warm, loving, perfect family life that escaped them in prior marriages/partnerships. They fantasize about stepparents easily and quickly replacing absent parents (i.e., instant love), about recreating the nuclear family, and about finding a partner who will share the financial responsibility and household workloads and bring them emotional security and love. Children often have different fantasies, wishing that their parents were still together or that they did not have to share their parent with the new stepparent. Some children may welcome a stepparent and may expect the stepparent to rescue them from poverty or loneliness. The task for stepfamilies is to bring to awareness unrealistic hopes and expectations, to articulate them, and to abandon them.

Immersion. At this stage the reality of stepfamily relationships hits home. When fantasies are not matched by experiences, stepfamily members become confused, and they have negative or ambivalent feelings for other family members. They may sense that things are not going as they should, that things do not feel right, or that something is wrong. Stepparents are often the first family member to be aware of these feelings and may blame themselves. It is in this stage that differing realities/experiences are first manifested between stepparents and biological parents, between adults and children, and between insiders and outsiders to family traditions and interaction patterns. The task for stepfamilies in this stage is to keep struggling through this period until family members can figure out what is wrong and can communicate with each other about their feelings and experiences.

Awareness. Papernow considers awareness to be the single most important stage. The tasks of this stage are to identify one's own feelings and needs and to try to understand the feelings and needs of others. Fantasies of how stepfamily relationships ought to be are replaced by more realistic perceptions of how these relationships may be different from those of first-marriage families. Some stepfamilies begin the stepfamily cycle at this stage or spend little time in immersion before entering awareness.

Mobilization. The task in the mobilization stage is to actively confront differences between family members and to constructively influence each other to make changes. This period may seem chaotic and full of stressful interactions over seemingly trivial issues, such as where the milk should be placed in the refrigerator or which adult's rules about table manners for children will prevail. These struggles are not trivial, however, and they are not over these minor issues. They are instead conflicts over fundamental changes in the way the stepfamily or relationships within it will function in the future. Conflicts over the placement of milk in the refrigerator or the proper use of a fork really may be conflicts over the stepparent's role and relationship vis-à-vis the children or over which of the minifamily's household rules will be the rules for the stepfamily household.

Action. Papernow (1993) subtitled the action stage "going into business together" (p. 384), and that is what happens for stepfamilies who reach this stage without dissolving. The developmental task is to generate new rituals, customs, and codes of conduct for relationships. New boundaries are drawn around steprelationships, and family members begin to figure out how to retain interaction patterns from previous families while developing new, more comfortable stepfamily relationships.

Contact. After the major changes in family interaction patterns of the middle stages, stepfamily relationships can begin to develop real intimacy and attachment. Tasks are to enjoy the "honeymoon" and to solidify further the stepparent role, which Papernow asserted begins to emerge clearly during this stage.

Resolution. Stepfamily norms have been established, there is a growing family history, and individual members have a sense of what their roles and relationships are. Step issues continue to arise, and during stressful periods there may be a recycling of stepfamily patterns from earlier stages. But relationships are secure enough that they are not threatened by conflicts or stressful encounters. The developmental task is to continue to work through grief and loss associated with earlier family changes/losses and loyalty conflicts.

The stepfamily cycle has received considerable favorable attention from clinicians since it was presented initially (Papernow, 1984). The model has intuitive appeal to clinicians, perhaps because it is a useful framework for conceptualizing individual and stepfamily developmental changes and perhaps because it also contains intervention suggestions appropriate for individuals and families.

Stepfamily Tasks

In addition to the developmental models just described, clinicians have proposed tasks that stepfamilies must master in their development toward being integrated units. Remarried families have to develop new patterns of interaction and eventually must develop a sense of identity as a family if they are to function successfully (Pill, 1990; Visher & Visher, 1988).

The Vishers identified eight tasks that must be addressed before stepfamilies can establish their own family identity (Visher & Visher, 1988). These tasks are based on problems that stepfamilies encounter as revealed in the clinical literature. A team of clinicians designed a self-help program around these tasks for the Stepfamily Association of America, called Stepfamilies Stepping Ahead (Burt, 1989). The tasks are as follows:

1. Dealing with losses and changes
2. Negotiating different developmental needs for different family members
3. Establishing new traditions
4. Developing a solid couple bond
5. Forming new relationships, particularly stepparent-stepchild bonds
6. Creating a parent coalition with former spouses
7. Accepting continual shifts in household composition
8. Risking involvement despite little support from society

The program is designed to help stepfamily adults explore more effective ways of establishing relationships by using a model of stepfamily dynamics, rather than nuclear family dynamics. In fact, Visher and Visher (1990) asserted that stepfamilies are successful to the degree they can master challenges in shifting from previous family cultures to a stepfamily culture. The Vishers identified six characteristics of successful stepfamilies: (a) losses have been mourned, (b) expectations are realistic, (c) the couple is strong and unified, (d) constructive rituals are established, (e) satisfactory steprelationships have formed, and (f) the separate households cooperate.

These tasks are not simple, nor are they easily or quickly completed. Some stepfamilies never successfully master any of the tasks. Other stepfamilies may accomplish certain tasks and fail miserably at others. It has been our experience that stepfamilies continue to work toward mastery of these tasks long after the children have grown up and left the household. Unlike first-marriage families, little is taken for granted in stepfamilies. Efforts to develop and maintain close relationships in remarried families are ongoing and challenging. Successes, because they may be hard-earned, can be unusually satisfying.

7

Epilogue
The Study of Remarried
Families in the 1990s

I t is still too early in this final decade of the century to assess what will happen regarding the study of close relationships in remarried families. Despite empirical evidence to the contrary, the image of the stepfamily as an extremely hostile environment for children remains (Popenoe, 1993). The strong tendency among many family scholars to view remarriage and stepfamily formation as a social problem and to view the traditional first-married nuclear family as the paradigm by which to judge all families continues.

In their 1989 book *The Sexual Bond: Rethinking Families and Close Relationships*, Scanzoni, Polonko, Teachman, and Thompson sug-

et al

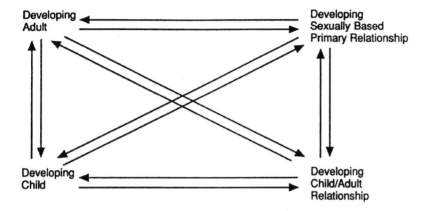

Figure 7.1. Ongoing Mutual Influences Among the Developing Sexually Based Primary Relationship, the Developing Adult, the Developing Child, and the Developing Child-Adult Relationship

SOURCE: From *The Sexual Bond: Rethinking Families and Close Relationships* (p. 168) by J. Scanzoni, K. Polonko, J. Teachman, & L. Thompson, 1989, Newbury Park, CA: Sage. Copyright © 1989 by Sage.

gested that the prevailing traditional family paradigm is in need of a fresh image. They asserted that the prevailing paradigm—that the traditional family is optimal—is "so strongly embedded that language/theory is structured to explain or to blame consequences, such as poverty, on women deviating from the ideal. Divorce, rather than structured economic dependence, becomes the villain" (p. 17). Remarriage, in turn, tends to be viewed as a response to the failure of an earlier marriage, rather than as an entity of its own.

Although not developed expressly for the study of remarriage, Scanzoni et al. suggested a new model as a starting place for reconceptualizing close relationships in families (see Figure 7.1). Primary or close relationships can be classified in at least four ways based on sex, friendship, blood, and propinquity. The higher order construct, sexually based primary relationship, replaces the lower order construct of marriage and alternative lifestyles. The sexual situation can be heterosexual, homosexual, multipartnered, and/or bisexual. As may be seen from the model, ongoing mutual influences are found among the developing sexually based primary relationship (which in the case of stepfamilies would be the remarried couple), the developing adult (i.e., the stepparent or the biological parent), the developing child, and the developing child-adult relationship (i.e., the stepchild-stepparent relationship or the child-parent relationship).

This model allows one to pursue the direct effects of one type of development (e.g., adult development) on the other three forms of development (e.g., child development, sexually based primary relationship development, and child-adult relationship development), yet also allows us to look at numerous indirect effects. For example, the developing adult (stepparent) influences the (step)child indirectly via his or her adult relationship (remarried couple) and also indirectly through the relationship the stepparent maintains with the stepchild. Simultaneously, the stepparent indirectly influences the parent via the stepchild and via the relationship the stepparent maintains with the stepchild. Additionally, the stepparent-stepchild relationship indirectly influences the stepparent via the remarried couple relationship and through changes in the stepchild. The stepchild also exercises indirect influences on the stepparent via the remarried couple relationship and via the relationship between the stepparent and the stepchild.

The preceding paragraph reflects some of the complexity typical in remarried families even though the example was quite simple. Additional children (i.e., siblings, stepsiblings, half-siblings) could be added to the model, as could additional parents (i.e., nonresidential biological parents, nonresidential stepparents). It is unlikely that one research design could test the entire model, but parts of the model can be investigated. The model then could be expanded and/or refined on the basis of empirical findings.

This model is obviously dynamic and is not based on the static view of family development that is characteristic of much family research. Neither is the model based on middle-class families, the focus of most family research and the overwhelming focus of stepfamily research. If family science continues to use static models and focuses narrowly on the American middle class, few gains will be made during the next decade in our understanding of the dynamics of stepfamilies.

We suggest additional directions the field should take that are compatible with the development and testing of more dynamic models of stepfamily development. Despite the dramatic increase in the quality and quantity of stepfamily research prior to 1990, in some areas there still is little published research. These areas include:

- descriptive studies of well-functioning stepfamilies, or investigations comparing the similarities and dissimilarities between functional stepfamily relationships and either functional nuclear family relationships or dysfunctional stepfamilies
- positive interpersonal relationships in stepfamilies
- the effects of the broader social environment on stepfamilies, including the interdependencies of stepfamilies and other social institutions (e.g., schools, the courts, religious institutions) and studies of the effects of mass media, public policy, and cultural stereotyping on remarriage and stepfamily interactions
- the role of individual family members' characteristics in mediating the quality of interpersonal and individual outcomes
- investigations of stepfamily systems, rather than stephouseholds only
- relationships following redivorce and multiple remarriages
- relationships within certain types of stephouseholds, such as stepmother households, and remarriages in which the children live elsewhere most of the time
- relationships within stepfamilies, such as interdependencies of subsystems within the stepfamily, relationships when older adults remarry, and stepsibling relations
- relationships in nonwhite stepfamily systems

In addition to the neglected areas mentioned above, a number of research methods and study designs have been underused. Research in remarriage and stepfamily dynamics in this decade should include:

- longitudinal studies that begin prior to remarriage
- studies using intragroup designs, rather than between-group comparisons
- single-stepfamily designs, borrowing the methods developed by psychologists and educators for the intensive examination of single subjects over time

- intervention studies employing either single-family designs or methods appropriate for larger samples
- the development of instruments specifically for assessing stepfamily dynamics and the development of norms for stepfamilies on well-known family instruments
- inductive theory-building efforts, the development of grounded theory, and other approaches that allow stepfamily members to instruct and inform researchers on important issues
- multilevel-multivariable designs
- tests of propositions from major and middle-range theories and from "partial theory" hypotheses
- multidisciplinary projects that combine research perspectives
- descriptive studies using detailed, reliable self-report and observational measures

Finally, the stepfamily can be identified as one of the protagonists of postmodern families. Stacey (1990) related that postmodern words create uneasiness in people. To some people the term *postmodern families* implies a radical transformation of familiar patterns of family activity and the emergence of new fields of family activity whose meanings and implications cannot yet be fathomed. Postmodern families are diverse, fluid, and unresolved. Stepfamilies, as representatives of postmodern families, are likely to continue to create uneasiness among people, including family scientists. The social stigma of stepfamilies also is likely to continue as a result of societal uneasiness with so-called nontraditional family forms.

Despite the uneasiness and stigma, stepfamilies continue to be formed, and stepfamily members continue to struggle with unresolved issues of how best to support family members. Because methods used successfully by first-married nuclear families are often not successful in stepfamilies, stepfamily members will continue to struggle, often failing, but also sometimes reaping successes as they carve out new patterns of interaction and new ways of being a family. In many ways stepfamilies can serve as laboratories for how families function. Things that seem natural in long-term first-married families must be worked out in sometimes awkward and painful fashion in remarried families. In learning any new skill, there is a period of practice, failure, more practice, and finally, it is hoped, success. It is hard to imagine from watching a child's first painful steps in learning to roller skate that the child soon will be zooming down the street, defying gravity and with a smile of triumph on his or her face. It also may be hard to imagine from watching the first painful steps in learning to be a stepparent or a stepchild that there will ever be a moment of triumph. Yet those moments exist for many. As we move into the postmodern era, it is important that we savor close relationships and interpersonal support and seek to better understand them. The stepfamily provides the perfect laboratory for such endeavors.

❦

References

Ahrons, C. R. (1980). Divorce: A crisis of family transition and change. *Family Relations, 29,* 533-540.

Ahrons, C. R., & Perlmutter, M. S. (1982). The relationship between former spouses: A fundamental subsystem in the remarriage family. In L. Messinger (Ed.), *Therapy with remarried families* (pp. 31-46). Rockville, MD: Aspen Systems.

Ahrons, C. R., & Rodgers, R. H. (1987). *Divorced families: A multidisciplinary developmental view.* New York: Norton.

Ahrons, C. R., & Wallisch, K. (1987). Parenting in the binuclear family: Relationships between biological and stepparents. In K. Pasley & M. Ihinger-Tallman (Eds.), *Remarriage and stepparenting today: Current research and theory* (pp. 225-256). New York: Guilford.

Albrecht, S. L. (1979). Correlates of marital happiness among the remarried. *Journal of Marriage and the Family, 41,* 857-867.

Amato, P. R. (1987). Family processes in one-parent, stepparent, and intact families: The child's point of view. *Journal of Marriage and the Family, 49,* 327-337.

Ambert, A. M. (1983). Separated women and remarriage behavior: A comparison of financially secure women and financially insecure women. *Journal of Divorce, 6,* 43-54.

Ambert, A. M. (1986). Being a stepparent: Live-in and visiting stepchildren. *Journal of Marriage and the Family, 48,* 795-804.

Ambert, A. M. (1988). Relationships with former in-laws after divorce: A research note. *Journal of Marriage and the Family, 50,* 679-686.

Ambert, A. M. (1989). *Ex-spouses and new spouses: A study of relationships.* Greenwich, CT: JAI.

Anderson, E. R., & Rice, A. M. (1992). Sibling relationships during remarriage. In E. M. Hetherington & G. Clingempeel (Eds.), *Coping with marital transitions.* Monographs of the Society for Research in Child Development, *57* (Serial No. 227), 149-177.

Anderson, J., & White, G. (1986). An empirical investigation of interactive and relationship patterns in functional and dysfunctional nuclear families and stepfamilies. *Family Process, 25,* 407-422.

Bachrach, C. A. (1983). Children in families: Characteristics of biological, step-, and adopted children. *Journal of Marriage and the Family, 45,* 171-179.

Bank, S. P., & Kahn, M. D. (1982). *The sibling bond.* New York: Basic Books.

Bateson, M. C. (1989). *Composing a life.* New York: Plume.

Baucom, D. H., & Epstein, N. (1990). *Cognitive-behavioral marital therapy.* New York: Brunner/Mazel.

Becker, G. S., Landis, E. M., & Michael, R. T. (1977). An economic analysis of marital instability. *Journal of Political Economy, 85,* 1141-1187.

Beer, W. R. (1992). *American stepfamilies.* New Brunswick, NJ: Transaction.

Bernard, J. (1956). *Remarriage: A study of marriage.* New York: Russell & Russell.

Bernard, J. (1972). *The future of marriage.* New York: Bantam.

Bernstein, A. (1989). *Yours, mine, and ours.* New York: Scribner.

Block, J., Block, J., & Gjerde, P. (1988). Parental functioning and the home environment in families of divorce: Prospective and concurrent analysis. *Journal of the American Academy of Child and Adolescent Psychiatry, 27,* 207-213.

Blumstein, P., & Schwartz, P. (1983). *American couples: Money, work, sex.* New York: Pocket Books.

Boer, F., & Dunn, J. (Eds.). (1992). *Children's sibling relationships: Developmental and clinical issues.* Hillsdale, NJ: Lawrence Erlbaum.

Bohannon, P. (1970). Divorce chains, households of remarriage, and multiple divorcers. In P. Bohannon (Ed.), *Divorce and after: An analysis of the emotional and social problems of divorce* (pp. 127-139). Garden City, NY: Doubleday.

Bohannon, P. (1984). Stepparenthood: A new and old experience. In R. S. Cohen, B. J. Cohler, & S. H. Weissman (Eds.), *Parenthood: A psychodynamic interpretation* (pp. 204-219). New York: Guilford.

Bohannon, P. (1985). *All the happy families*. New York: McGraw-Hill.

Booth, A., Brinkerhoff, D., & White, L. (1984). The impact of parental divorce on courtship. *Journal of Marriage and the Family, 46*, 85-94.

Booth, A., & Edwards, J. N. (1992). Starting over: Why remarriages are more unstable. *Journal of Family Issues, 13*, 179-194.

Boss, P., & Greenberg, J. (1984). Family boundary ambiguity: A new variable in family stress theory. *Family Process, 23*, 535-546.

Bowerman, C. E., & Irish, D. (1962). Some relationships of stepchildren to their parents. *Marriage and Family Living, 24*, 113-121.

Bradbury, T. N., & Fincham, F. D. (1988). Individual difference variables in close relationships: A contextual model of marriage as an integrative framework. *Journal of Personality and Social Psychology, 54*, 713-721.

Bradbury, T. N., & Fincham, F. D. (1990). Attributions in marriage: Review and critique. *Psychological Bulletin, 107*, 3-33.

Braver, S. L., Wolchik, S. A., Sandler, I. N., & Sheets, V. L. (1993). A social exchange model of nonresidential parent involvement. In C. Depner & J. Bray (Eds.), *Nonresidential parenting: New vistas in family living* (pp. 87-108). Newbury Park, CA: Sage.

Bray, J. (1992). Family relationships and children's adjustment in clinical and nonclinical stepfather families. *Journal of Family Psychology, 6*, 60-68.

Bray, J., Berger, S. H., Silverblatt, A. H., & Hollier, A. (1987). Family process and organization during early remarriage: A preliminary analysis. In J. P. Vincent (Ed.), *Advances in family intervention, assessment, and theory* (pp. 253-279). Greenwich, CT: JAI.

Bray, J., & Depner, C. (1993). Perspectives on nonresidential parenting. In C. Depner & J. Bray (Eds.), *Nonresidential parenting: New vistas in family living* (pp. 3-12). Newbury Park, CA: Sage.

Brody, G. H., Neubaum, E., & Forehand, R. (1988). Serial marriage: A heuristic analysis of an emerging family form. *Psychological Bulletin, 103*, 211-222.

Brown, A. C., Green, R. J., & Druckman, J. (1990). A comparison of stepfamilies with and without child-focused problems. *American Journal of Orthopsychiatry, 60*, 556-566.

Brown, K. (1987). Stepmothering: Myth and realities. *Affilia, 2*, 34-45.

Bumpass, L. L. (1984). Some characteristics of children's second families. *American Journal of Sociology, 90*, 608-623.

Bumpass, L. L. (1990). What's happening to the family? Interactions between demographic and institutional change. *Demography, 27*, 483-498.

Bumpass, L. L., & Sweet, J. A. (1989). National estimates of cohabitation: Cohort levels and union stability. *Demography, 26*, 615-625.

Bumpass, L. L., Sweet, J. A., & Castro Martin, T. (1990). Changing patterns of remarriage. *Journal of Marriage and the Family, 52*, 747-756.

Burgoyne, J., & Clark, D. (1984). *Making a go of it: A study of stepfamilies in Sheffield*. Boston: Routledge & Kegan Paul.

Burt, M. (Ed.). (1989). *Stepfamilies stepping ahead.* Lincoln, NE: Stepfamily Association of America.

Byrd, A., & Smith, R. (1988). A qualitative analysis of the decision to remarry using Gilligan's ethic of care. *Journal of Divorce, 11,* 87-102.

Carter, E. A. (1988). Counseling stepfamilies effectively. *Behavior Today, 19,* 1-2.

Castro Martin, T. C., & Bumpass, L. L. (1989). Recent trends in marital disruption. *Demography, 26,* 37-51.

Cate, R. M., & Lloyd, S. A. (1992). *Courtship.* Newbury Park, CA: Sage.

Chambers, D. L. (1990). Stepparents, biologic parents, and the law's perceptions of "family" after divorce. In S. D. Sugarman & H. H. Kay (Eds.), *Divorce reform at the crossroads* (pp. 102-129). New Haven, CT: Yale University Press.

Chamie, J., & Nsuly, S. (1981). Sex differences in remarriage and spouse selection. *Demography, 18,* 335-348.

Chandler, J. (1991). *Women without husbands: An exploration of the margins of marriage.* New York: St. Martin's.

Cherlin, A. (1978). Remarriage as an incomplete institution. *American Journal of Sociology, 84,* 634-650.

Cherlin, A., & Furstenberg, F. (1986). *American grandparenthood.* New York: Basic Books.

Cherlin, A., & McCarthy, J. (1985). Remarried couple households: Data from the June 1980 Current Population Survey. *Journal of Marriage and the Family, 47,* 23-30.

Cicirelli, V. (in press). Sibling relationships in cross-cultural perspective. *Journal of Marriage and the Family.*

Cissna, K. N., Cox, D. E., & Bochner, A. P. (1990). The dialectic of marital and parental relationships within the stepfamily. *Communication Monographs, 57*(1), 44-61.

Clingempeel, W. G. (1981). Quasi-kin relationships and marital quality. *Journal of Personality and Social Psychology, 41,* 890-901.

Clingempeel, W. G., & Brand, E. (1985). Quasi-kin relationships, structural complexity, and marital quality in stepfamilies: A replication, extension, and clinical implications. *Family Relations, 34,* 401-409.

Clingempeel, W. G., Brand, E., & Segal, S. (1987). A multilevel-multivariable-developmental perspective for future research on stepfamilies. In K. Pasley & M. Ihinger-Tallman (Eds.), *Remarriage and stepparenting today: Current research and theory* (pp. 65-93). New York: Guilford.

Clingempeel, W. G., Colyar, J., Brand, E., & Hetherington, E. M. (1992). Children's relationships with maternal grandparents: A longitudinal study of family structure and pubertal status effects. *Child Development, 63,* 1404-1422.

Clingempeel, W. G., Flescher, M., & Brand, E. (1987). Research on stepfamilies: Paradigmatic constraints and alternative proposals. In J. P. Vincent (Ed.), *Advances in family intervention: Assessment and theory* (pp. 229-251). Greenwich, CT: JAI.

Clingempeel, W. G., & Segal, S. (1986). Stepparent-stepchild relationships and the psychological adjustment of children in stepmother and stepfather families. *Child Development, 57,* 474-484.

Coale Lewis, H. C. (1985). Family therapy with stepfamilies. *Journal of Strategic and Systemic Therapies, 4,* 13-23.

Coleman, M., & Ganong, L. (1984). Effect of family structure on family attitudes and expectations. *Family Relations, 33,* 425-432.

Coleman, M., & Ganong, L. (1985). Remarriage myths: Implications for the helping professions. *Journal of Counseling and Development, 64,* 116-120.

Coleman, M., & Ganong, L. (1986a). *Bibliotherapy with stepfamilies.* Springfield, IL: Charles C Thomas.

Coleman, M., & Ganong, L. (1986b, November). *Stepchildren: Empirical examination of some clinical assumptions.* Paper presented at the Annual Conference of the National Council on Family Relations, Dearborn, MI.

Coleman, M., & Ganong, L. (1987a). The cultural stereotyping of stepfamilies. In K. Pasley & M. Ihinger-Tallman (Eds.), *Remarriage and stepparenting today: Current research and theory* (pp. 19-41). New York: Guilford.

Coleman, M., & Ganong, L. (1987b). Marital conflict in stepfamilies: Effects on children. *Youth and Society, 19,* 151-172.

Coleman, M., & Ganong, L. (1989). Financial management in stepfamilies. *Lifestyles: Family and Economic Issues, 10,* 217-232.

Coleman, M., & Ganong, L. (1990). Remarriage and stepfamily research in the 80s: New interest in an old family form. *Journal of Marriage and the Family, 52,* 925-940.

Coleman, M., Ganong, L., & Henry, J. (1984a, October/December). Children and stepfamilies. *Leadership,* pp. 6-7.

Coleman, M., Ganong, L., & Henry, J. (1984b). What teachers should know about stepfamilies. *Childhood Education, 60,* 306-309.

Collins, S. (1991). The transition from lone parent family to stepfamily. In M. Hardey & G. Crow (Eds.), *Lone parenthood: Coping with constraints and making opportunities in single-parent families* (pp. 156-174). Toronto: University of Toronto Press.

Coontz, S. (1992). *The way we never were.* New York: Basic Books.

Counts, R. M. (1992). Second and third divorces: The flood to come. *Journal of Divorce and Remarriage, 17,* 193-200.

Crane, D. (1972). *Invisible colleges: Diffusion of knowledge in scientific communities.* Chicago: University of Chicago Press.

Crosbie-Burnett, M. (1984). The centrality of the step relationship: A challenge to family theory and practice. *Family Relations, 33,* 459-464.

Crosbie-Burnett, M. (1988). Impact of joint versus maternal legal custody, sex and age of adolescent, and family structure complexity on adolescents in remarried families. *Conciliation Courts Review, 26,* 47-52.

Crosbie-Burnett, M. (1989a). Application of family stress theory to remarriage: A model for assessing and helping stepfamilies. *Family Relations, 38,* 323-331.

Crosbie-Burnett, M. (1989b). Impact of custody arrangement and family structure on remarriage. *Journal of Divorce, 13*, 1-16.

Crosbie-Burnett, M., & Giles-Sims, J. (1991). Marital power in stepfather families: A test of normative-resource theory. *Journal of Family Psychology, 4*, 484-496.

Crosbie-Burnett, M., Skyles, A., & Becker-Haven, J. (1988). Exploring stepfamilies from a feminist perspective. In S. Dornbusch & M. Strober (Eds.), *Feminism, children, and new families* (pp. 297-326). New York: Guilford.

Daly, M., & Wilson, M. (1980). Discriminative parental solicitude: A biological perspective. *Journal of Marriage and the Family, 42*, 277-288.

Day, R. D., & Bahr, S. J. (1986). Income changes following divorce and remarriage. *Journal of Divorce, 9*, 75-88.

Dean, G., & Gurak, D. T. (1978). Marital homogamy the second time around. *Journal of Marriage and the Family, 40*, 559-570.

Demo, D. H., & Acock, A. C. (1993). Family diversity and the division of domestic labor: How much have things really changed? *Family Relations, 42*, 323-331.

Dornbusch, S. M., Ritter, P. L., Leiderman, P. H., Roberts, D. F., & Fraleigh, M. J. (1987). The relation of parenting style to adolescent school performance. *Child Development, 58*, 1244-1257.

Duberman, L. (1975). *The reconstituted family: A study of remarried couples and their children.* Chicago: Nelson-Hall.

Ellis, A., & Grieger, R. (Eds.). (1977). *Handbook of rational-emotive therapy.* New York: Springer.

Emery, R. E. (1988). *Marriage, divorce, and children's adjustment.* Newbury Park, CA: Sage.

Espinoza, R., & Newman, Y. (1979). *Stepparenting* (DHEW Publication No. 48-579). Rockville, MD: U.S. Department of Health, Education, and Welfare.

Esses, L., & Campbell, R. (1984). Challenges in researching the remarried. *Family Relations, 33*, 415-424.

Farrell, J., & Markman, H. (1986). Individual and interpersonal factors in the etiology of marital distress: The example of remarital couples. In R. Gilmour & S. Duck (Eds.), *The emerging field of personal relationships* (pp. 251-263). Hillsdale, NJ: Lawrence Erlbaum.

Fast, I., & Cain, A. C. (1966). The stepparent role: Potential for disturbances in family functioning. *American Journal of Orthopsychiatry, 36*, 435-441.

Ferri, E. (1984). *Stepchildren: A national study.* Atlantic Highlands, NJ: Humanities Press.

Filinson, R. (1986). Relationships in stepfamilies—An examination of alliances. *Journal of Comparative Family Studies, 17*, 43-62.

Fine, M. A. (1986). Perceptions of stepparents: Variation in stereotypes as a function of current family structure. *Journal of Marriage and the Family, 48*, 537-543.

Fine, M. A., Donnelly, B., & Voydanoff, P. (1991). The relation between adolescents' perceptions of their family lives and their adjustment in stepfather families. *Journal of Adolescent Research, 6*, 424.

Fine, M. A., & Fine, D. R. (1992). Recent changes in laws affecting stepfamilies: Suggestions for legal reform. *Family Relations, 41,* 334-340.

Fine, M. A., & Schwebel, A. I. (1991). Stepparent stress: A cognitive perspective. *Journal of Divorce and Remarriage, 17,* 1-15.

Finkelhor, D. (1987). The sexual abuse of children: Current research reviewed. *Psychiatric Annals, 17,* 233-241.

Fisher, H. E. (1989). Evolution of human serial pairbonding. *American Journal of Physical Anthropology, 78,* 331-354.

Fishman, B., & Hamel, B. (1981). From nuclear to stepfamily ideology: A stressful change. *Alternative Lifestyles, 4,* 181-204.

Flinn, M. (1988). Step- and genetic parent/offspring relationships in a Caribbean village. *Ethology and Sociobiology, 9,* 335-369.

Flinn, M. (1992). Paternal care in a Caribbean village. In B. S. Hewlett (Ed.), *Father-child relations: Cultural and biosocial contexts* (pp. 57-84). Hawthorne, NY: Aldine.

Folk, K. F., Graham, J. W., & Beller, A. H. (1992). Child support and remarriage: Implications for the economic well-being of children. *Journal of Family Issues, 13,* 142-157.

Fox, G. L., & Inazu, J. K. (1982). The influence of mother's marital history on the mother-daughter relationship in black and white households. *Journal of Marriage and the Family, 44,* 143-153.

Funder, K. (1991). Children's constructions of their postdivorce families: A family sculpture approach. In K. Funder (Ed.), *Images of Australian families* (pp. 73-101). Melbourne: Longman Cheshire.

Furstenberg, F. F., Jr. (1979). Recycling the family: Perspectives for a neglected family form. *Marriage and Family Review, 2*(3), 1, 12-22.

Furstenberg, F. F. (1987). The new extended family: The experience of parents and children after remarriage. In K. Pasley & M. Ihinger-Tallman (Eds.), *Remarriage and stepparenting today: Current research and theory* (pp. 42-61). New York: Guilford.

Furstenberg, F. F. (1988). Child care after divorce and remarriage. In E. M. Hetherington & J. D. Arasteh (Eds.), *Impact of divorce, single parenting, and stepparenting* (pp. 245-261). Hillsdale, NJ: Lawrence Erlbaum.

Furstenberg, F. F., Jr., & Cherlin, A. J. (1991). *Divided families: What happens to children when parents part.* Cambridge, MA: Harvard University Press.

Furstenberg, F. F., Jr., & Nord, C. W. (1985). Parenting apart: Patterns of childrearing after marital disruption. *Journal of Marriage and the Family, 47,* 893-904.

Furstenberg, F. F., Jr., & Spanier, G. (1984). *Recycling the family: Remarriage after divorce.* Beverly Hills, CA: Sage.

Galinsky, E. (1981). *Between generations, the six stages of parenthood.* New York: Times Books.

Ganong, L. (1993). Family diversity in a youth organization: Involvement of single-parents families and stepfamilies in 4-H. *Family Relations, 42,* 286-292.

Ganong, L., & Coleman, M. (1983). Stepparent: A pejorative term? *Psychological Reports, 52*, 919-922.

Ganong, L., & Coleman, M. (1984). Effects of remarriage on children: A review of the empirical literature. *Family Relations, 33*, 389-406.

Ganong, L., & Coleman, M. (1986). A comparison of clinical and empirical literature on children in stepfamilies. *Journal of Marriage and the Family, 48*, 309-318.

Ganong, L., & Coleman, M. (1987). Effects of parental remarriage on children: An updated comparison of theories, methods, and findings from clinical and empirical research. In K. Pasley & M. Ihinger-Tallman (Eds.), *Remarriage and stepparenting today: Current research and theory* (pp. 94-140). New York: Guilford.

Ganong, L., & Coleman, M. (1988). Do mutual children cement bonds in stepfamilies? *Journal of Marriage and the Family, 50*, 687-698.

Ganong, L., & Coleman, M. (1989). Preparing for remarriage: Anticipating the issues, seeking solutions. *Family Relations, 38*, 28-33.

Ganong, L., & Coleman, M. (1992). Gender differences in self and future partner expectations. *Journal of Family Issues, 13*, 55-64.

Ganong, L., & Coleman, M. (in press). Adolescent-stepchild-stepparent relationships: Changes over time. In K. Pasley & M. Ihinger-Tallman (Eds.), *Stepparenting: Issues in theory, research, and practice.*

Ganong, L., Coleman, M., & Brown, G. (1981). Effects of family structure on marital attitudes of adolescents. *Adolescence, 16*, 281-288.

Ganong, L., Coleman, M., & Fine, M. (in press). Remarriage and stepfamilies. In W. Burr & R. Day (Eds.), *Advanced family science.* Provo, UT: BYU.

Ganong, L., Coleman, M., & Kennedy, G. (1990). The effects of using alternate labels in denoting stepparent or stepfamily status. *Journal of Social Behavior and Personality, 5*, 453-463.

Ganong, L., Coleman, M., & Mapes, D. (1990). A meta-analytic review of family structure stereotypes. *Journal of Marriage and the Family, 52*, 287-298.

Gelles, R. J. (1980). Violence in the family: A review of research in the seventies. *Journal of Marriage and the Family, 42*, 873-885.

Gelles, R. J., & Harrop, J. W. (1991). The risk of abusive violence among children with nongenetic caretakers. *Family Relations, 40*, 78-83.

Gergen, K. J. (1985). The social constructionist movement in modern psychology. *American Psychologist, 40*, 266-275.

Gerstel, N. (1987). Divorce and stigma. *Social Problems, 34*, 172-186.

Gil, D. (1970). *Violence against children.* Cambridge, MA: Harvard University Press.

Giles-Sims, J. (1984). The stepparent role: Expectations, behavior, sanctions. *Journal of Family Issues, 5*, 116-130.

Giles-Sims, J. (1987a). Parental role sharing between remarrieds and ex-spouses. *Youth and Society, 19*, 134-150.

Giles-Sims, J. (1987b). Social exchange in remarried families. In K. Pasley & M. Ihinger-Tallman (Eds.), *Remarriage and stepparenting today: Research and theory* (pp. 141-163). New York: Guilford.

Giles-Sims, J., & Crosbie-Burnett, M. (1989). Adolescent power in stepfather families: A test of normative resource theory. *Journal of Marriage and the Family, 51,* 1065-1078.

Giles-Sims, J., & Finkelhor, D. (1984). Child abuse in stepfamilies. *Family Relations, 33,* 407-414.

Glick, P. (1989). Remarried families, stepfamilies, and stepchildren: A brief demographic analysis. *Family Relations, 38,* 24-27.

Glick, P. C. (1980). Remarriage: Some recent changes and variations. *Journal of Family Issues, 1,* 455-478.

Glick, P. C. (1984). Marriage, divorce, and living arrangements: Prospective changes. *Journal of Family Issues, 5,* 7-26.

Goetting, A. (1979). The normative integration of the former spouse relationship. *Journal of Divorce, 2,* 395-414.

Goetting, A. (1980). Former spouse-current spouse relationships. *Journal of Family Issues, 1,* 58-80.

Goetting, A. (1982). The six stations of remarriage: Developmental tasks of remarriage after divorce. *Family Relations, 31,* 213-222.

Goldner, V. (1982). Remarriage family: Structure, system, future. In J. C. Hansen & L. Messinger (Eds.), *Therapy with remarried families* (pp. 187-206). Rockville, MD: Aspen.

Goode, W. J. (1956). *After divorce.* Glencoe, IL: Free Press.

Goode, W. J. (1963). *World revolution and family patterns.* New York: Free Press.

Gordon, M., & Creighton, S. (1988). Natal and nonnatal fathers as sexual abusers in the United Kingdom: A comparative analysis. *Journal of Marriage and the Family, 50,* 99-105.

Gross, P. E. (1987). Defining postdivorce remarriage families: A typology based on the subjective perceptions of children. *Journal of Divorce, 10,* 205-217.

Guisinger, S., Cowan, P., & Schuldberg, D. (1989). Changing parent and spouse relations in the first years of remarriage of divorced fathers. *Journal of Marriage and the Family, 51,* 445-456.

Halliday, T. (1980). Remarriage: The more compleat institution. *American Journal of Sociology, 86,* 630-635.

Halperin, S., & Smith, T. (1983). Differences in stepchildren's perceptions of their stepfathers and natural fathers: Implications for family therapy. *Journal of Divorce, 7,* 19-30.

Hanna, S. L., & Knaub, P. K. (1984). Cohabitation before remarriage: Its relationship to family strengths. *Alternative Lifestyles, 4,* 507-522.

Hendrick, S. S., & Hendrick, C. (1992). *Liking, loving, and relating* (2nd ed.). Belmont, CA: Brooks/Cole.

Henry, C. S., Ceglian, C. P., & Ostrander, D. L. (1993). The transition to stepgrandparenthood. *Journal of Divorce and Remarriage, 19,* 25-44.

Hetherington, E. M. (1987). Family relations six years after divorce. In K. Pasley & M. Ihinger-Tallman (Eds.), *Remarriage and stepparenting today: Current research and theory* (pp. 185-205). New York: Guilford.

Hetherington, E. M., & Clingempeel, W. G. (1992). Coping with marital transitions: A family systems perspective. *Monographs of the Society for Research in Child Development, 57*(2-3, Serial No. 227).

Hetherington, E. M., Cox, M., & Cox, R. (1985). Long-term effects of divorce and remarriage on the adjustment of children. *Journal of the American Academy of Child Psychiatry, 24,* 518-530.

Hill, R. (1986). Life cycle stages for types of single parent families: A family development theory. *Family Relations, 35,* 19-29.

Hobart, C. (1989). Experiences of remarried families. *Journal of Divorce, 13,* 121-144.

Hobart, C. (1991). Conflict in remarriages. *Journal of Divorce and Remarriage, 15,* 69-86.

Hobart, C. W. (1987). Parent-child relations in remarried families. *Journal of Family Issues, 8*(3), 259-277.

Hobart, C. W. (1988). Perception of parent-child relationships in first-married and remarried families. *Family Relations, 37*(2), 175-182.

Hoffman, L. W. (1991). The influence of the family environment on personality: Accounting for sibling differences. *Psychological Bulletin, 110,* 187-203.

Hoffman, S. D., & Duncan, G. J. (1988). What are the economic consequences of divorce? *Demography, 25,* 641-645.

Holman, T. B., & Burr, W. R. (1980). Beyond the beyond: The growth of family theories in the 1970s. *Journal of Marriage and the Family, 42,* 729-741.

Howe, N. (1986). *Socialization, social cognitive factors, and the development of the sibling relationship.* Unpublished doctoral dissertation, University of Waterloo, Waterloo, Canada.

Ihinger-Tallman, M. (1987). Sibling and stepsibling bonding in stepfamilies. In K. Pasley & M. Ihinger-Tallman (Eds.), *Remarriage and stepparenting today: Current research and theory* (pp. 164-184). New York: Guilford.

Ihinger-Tallman, M. (1988). Research on stepfamilies. *Annual Reviews of Sociology, 14,* 25-48.

Ihinger-Tallman, M., & Pasley, K. (1987a). Divorce and remarriage in the American family: An historical overview. In K. Pasley & M. Ihinger-Tallman (Eds.), *Remarriage and stepparenting today: Current research and theory* (pp. 3-18). New York: Guilford.

Ihinger-Tallman, M., & Pasley, K. (1987b). *Remarriage.* Newbury Park, CA: Sage.

Imber-Black, E., & Roberts, J. (1993). *Rituals for our times.* New York: Harper Perennial.

Ishii-Kuntz, M., & Coltrane, S. (1992). Remarriage, stepparenting, and household labor. *Journal of Family Issues, 13,* 215-233.

Jacobson, D. S. (1987). Family type, visiting, and children's behavior in the stepfamily: A linked family system. In K. Pasley & M. Ihinger-Tallman (Eds.), *Remarriage and stepparenting today: Current research and theory* (pp. 257-272). New York: Guilford.

Johnson, C. L. (1988). Postdivorce reorganization of relationships between divorcing children and their parents. *Journal of Marriage and the Family, 50,* 221-231.

Kalmuss, D., & Seltzer, J. A. (1986). Continuity of marital behavior in remarriage: The case of spouse abuse. *Journal of Marriage and the Family, 48,* 113-120.

Kalmuss, D., & Seltzer, J. A. (1989). A framework for studying socialization over the life cycle: The case of family violence. *Journal of Family Issues, 10,* 339-358.

Kaplan, L., & Hennon, C. B. (1992). Remarriage education: The personal reflections program. *Family Relations, 41,* 127-134.

Keen, S. (1983). *The passionate life: Stages of loving.* New York: Harper & Row.

Kennedy, G. (1985). Family relationships as perceived by college students from single-parent, blended, and intact families. *Family Perspective, 19,* 117-126.

Kiecolt, K. J., & Acock, A. C. (1988). The long-term effects of family structure on gender-role attitudes. *Journal of Marriage and the Family, 50,* 709-717.

Kinnaird, K. L., & Gerrard, M. (1986). Premarital sexual behavior and attitudes toward marriage and divorce among young women as a function of their mother's marital status. *Journal of Marriage and the Family, 48,* 757-765.

Koepke, L., Hare, J., & Moran, P. B. (1992). Relationship quality in a sample of lesbian couples with children and child-free lesbian couples. *Family Relations, 41,* 224-229.

Kompara, D. R. (1980). Difficulties in the socialization of stepparenting. *Family Relations, 29,* 69-73.

Koo, H. P., & Suchindran, C. M. (1980). Effects of children on women's remarriage prospects. *Journal of Family Issues, 1,* 497-515.

Koo, H. P., Suchindran, C. M., & Griffith, J. D. (1984). The effects of children on divorce and remarriage: A multivariate analysis of life table probabilities. *Population Studies, 38,* 451.

Kurdek, L. (1990). Divorce history and self-reported psychological distress in husbands and wives. *Journal of Marriage and the Family, 52,* 701-708.

Kurdek, L. (1991a). Marital stability and changes in marital quality in newly wed couples: A test of the contextual model. *Journal of Social and Personal Relationships, 8,* 27-48.

Kurdek, L. (1991b). Predictors of increases in marital distress in newlywed couples: A 3-year prospective longitudinal study. *Developmental Psychology, 27,* 627-636.

Kurdek, L., & Fine. M. (1991). Cognitive correlates of satisfaction for mothers and stepfathers in stepfather families. *Journal of Marriage and the Family, 53,* 565-572.

Kurdek, L., & Fine, M. (1993). The relation between family structure and young adolescents' appraisals of family climate and parenting behavior. *Journal of Family Issues, 14,* 279-290.

Kvanli, J. A., & Jennings, G. (1987). Recoupling: Development and establishment of the spousal subsystem in remarriage. *Journal of Divorce, 10,* 189-203.

Landis, P. (1950). Sequential marriage. *Journal of Home Economics, 42,* 625-628.

Larson, J. H., & Allgood, S. M. (1987). A comparison of intimacy in first-married and remarried couples. *Journal of Family Issues, 8,* 319-331.

Leslie, G. (1976). *The family in social context.* New York: Oxford University Press.

Leslie, L. A., & Epstein, N. (1988). Cognitive-behavioral treatment of remarried families. In N. Epstein, S. E. Schlesinger, & W. Dryden (Eds.), *Cognitive-behavioral therapy with families* (pp. 151-182). New York: Brunner/Mazel.

Lightcap, J. L., Kurland, J. A., & Burgess, R. L. (1982). Child abuse: A test of some predictions from evolutionary theory. *Ethology and Sociobiology, 3,* 61-67.

Lopata, H. Z. (1979). *Women as widows: Support systems.* New York: Elsevier.

Lutz, P. (1983). The stepfamily: An adolescent perspective. *Family Relations, 32,* 367-376.

Malkin, C., & Lamb, M. (1989). *Child maltreatment: A test of sociobiology theory.* Unpublished manuscript.

Margolin, L. (1992). Child abuse by mothers' boyfriends: Why the overrepresentation? *Child Abuse & Neglect, 16,* 541-551.

Martin, D., Martin, M., & Jeffers, P. (1993). *Stepfamilies in therapy.* San Francisco: Jossey-Bass.

McCarthy, J. (1978). A comparison of the probability of the dissolution of first and second marriages. *Demography, 15,* 345-359.

McCranie, E. W., & Kahan, J. (1986). Personality and multiple divorce: A prospective study. *Journal of Nervous and Mental Disease, 174*(3), 161-164.

McGoldrick, M., & Carter, E. A. (1989). Forming a remarried family. In E. A. Carter & M. McGoldrick (Eds.), *The family cycle: A framework for family therapy* (pp. 399-429). New York: Gardner.

McKenry, P. C., & Price, S. J. (1991). Alternatives for support: Life after divorce—A literature review. *Journal of Divorce and Remarriage, 15*(3-4), 1-19.

McLanahan, S., & Bumpass, L. (1988). Intergenerational consequences of family disruption. *American Journal of Sociology, 94,* 130-152.

Mead, M. (1970). Anomalies in American postdivorce relationships. In P. Bohannon (Ed.), *Divorce and after: An analysis of the emotional and social problems of divorce* (pp. 107-125). Garden City, NY: Doubleday.

Messinger, L. (1976). Remarriage between divorced people with children from previous marriages: A proposal for preparation for remarriage. *Journal of Marriage and Family Counseling, 2,* 193-200.

Messinger, L., Walker, L. N., & Freeman, S. J. J. (1978). Preparation for remarriage following divorce: The use of group techniques. *American Journal of Orthopsychiatry, 48,* 263-272.

Michael, R., & Tuma, N. (1985). Entry into marriage and parenthood by young men and women: The influence of family background. *Demography, 22,* 515-544.

Miller, B. C. (1993). Families, science, and values. *Journal of Marriage and the Family, 55,* 7-22.

Miller, J., & Schreiner, T. (1992, January 20). Single dads lead more families. *San Francisco Chronicle,* pp. 1, 4.

Mills, D. (1984). A model for stepfamily development. *Family Relations, 33,* 365-372.

Minuchin, S. (1974). *Families and family therapy.* Cambridge, MA: Harvard University Press.

Minuchin, S., & Nichols, M. P. (1993). *Family healing.* New York: Free Press.

Montgomery, M. J., Anderson, E. R., Hetherington, E. M., & Clingempeel, W. G. (1992). Patterns of courtship for remarriage: Implications for child adjustment and parent-child relationships. *Journal of Marriage and the Family, 54,* 686-698.

Morrison, K., & Thompson-Guppy, A. (1985). Cinderella's stepmother syndrome. *Canadian Journal of Psychiatry, 30,* 521-529.

Mott, F. L., & Moore, S. F. (1983). The tempo of remarriage among young American women. *Journal of Marriage and the Family, 45,* 427-435.

National Center for Health Statistics. (1993). *1988 marriages: Number of the marriage of bride by groom* [Computer program]. Washington, DC: NCHS Computer Center.

Nelson, W. P., & Levant, R. F. (1991). An evaluation of a skills training program for parents in stepfamilies. *Family Relations, 40,* 291-296.

Noy, D. (1991). Wicked stepmothers in Roman society and imagination. *Journal of Family History, 16,* 345-361.

O'Flaherty, K., & Eells, L. (1988). Courtship behavior of the remarried. *Journal of Marriage and the Family, 50,* 499-506.

Oh, S. (1986). Remarried men and remarried women: How are they different? *Journal of Divorce, 9,* 107-113.

Orleans, M., Palisi, B., & Caddell, D. (1989). Marriage adjustment and satisfaction of stepfathers: Their feelings and perceptions of decision-making and stepchildren relations. *Family Relations, 38,* 371-377.

Palisi, B. J., Orleans, M., Caddell, D., & Korn, B. (1991). Adjustment to stepfatherhood: The effects of marital history and relations with children. *Journal of Divorce and Remarriage, 14,* 89-106

Papernow, P. (1993). *Becoming a stepfamily: Patterns of development in remarried families.* New York: Gardner.

Papernow, P. L. (1984). The stepfamily cycle: An experimental model of stepfamily development. *Family Relations, 33,* 355-364.

Papernow, P. L. (1987). Thickening the "middle ground": Dilemmas and vulnerabilities of remarried couples. *Psychotherapy, 24,* 630-639.

Pasley, K. (1987). Family boundary ambiguity: Perceptions of adult remarried family members. In K. Pasley & M. Ihinger-Tallman (Eds.), *Remarriage and stepparenting today: Current research and theory* (pp. 206-224). New York: Guilford.

Pasley, K., & Ihinger-Tallman, M. (1982). Remarried family life: Supports and constraints. In G. Rowe (Ed.), *Building family strengths 4* (pp. 367-383). Lincoln: University of Nebraska Press.

Pasley, K., & Ihinger-Tallman, M. (1987). *Remarriage and stepparenting today: Current research and theory.* New York: Guilford.

Pasley, K., & Ihinger-Tallman, M. (1992). Remarriage and stepparenting: What the 1980s have added to our understanding of these families. *Family Science Review, 5,* 153-174.

Peek, C. W., Bell, N. J., Waldren, T., & Sorell, G. (1988). Patterns of functioning in families of remarried and first married couples. *Journal of Marriage and the Family, 50,* 699-708.

Pill, C. J. (1981). A family life education group for working with stepparents. *Social Casework, 62,* 159-166.

Pill, C. J. (1990). Stepfamilies: Redefining the family. *Family Relations, 39,* 186-193.

Pink, J. E., & Wampler, K. S. (1985). Problem areas in stepfamilies: Cohesion, adaptability, and the stepfather-adolescent relationship. *Family Relations, 34,* 327-335.

Popenoe, D. (1993, October). *The evaluation of marriage and the problem of stepfamilies.* Paper presented at the National Symposium on Stepfamilies: Who Benefits? Who Does Not? University Park, PA.

Price, S., & McKenry, P. (1988). *Divorce.* Newbury Park, CA: Sage.

Price-Bonham, S., & Balswick, J. O. (1980). The noninstitutions: Divorce, desertion, and remarriage. *Journal of Marriage and the Family, 42,* 959-972.

Ramsey, S. H. (1986). Stepparent support of stepchildren: The changing legal context and the need for empirical policy research. *Family Relations, 35,* 363-369.

Ransom, J. W., Schlesinger, S., & Derdeyn, A. P. (1979). A stepfamily in formation. *American Journal of Orthopsychiatry, 49,* 36-43.

Roberts, T. W., & Price, S. J. (1987). Instant families: Divorced mothers marry never-married men. *Journal of Divorce, 11*(1), 71-92.

Roberts, T. W., & Price, S. J. (1989). Adjustment in remarriage: Communication, cohesion, marital, and parental roles. *Journal of Divorce, 13*(1), 17-43.

Robinson, M. (1991). *Family transformation through divorce and remarriage: A systematic approach.* New York: Routledge, Chapman, & Hall.

Rodgers, R. H., & Conrad, L. (1986). Courtship for remarriage: Influences on family reorganization after divorce. *Journal of Marriage and the Family, 48,* 767-775.

Rosenberg, E. B., & Hajfal, F. (1985). Stepsibling relationships in remarried families. *Social Casework: The Journal of Contemporary Social Work, 66,* 287-292.

Russell, D. E. (1984). The prevalence and seriousness of incestuous abuse: Stepfathers vs. biological fathers. *Child Abuse & Neglect, 8,* 15-22.

Sager, C. J., Brown, H. S., Crohn, H., Engel, T., Rodstein, E., & Walker, E. (1983). *Treating the remarried family.* New York: Brunner/Mazel.

Sager, C. J., Walker, E., Brown, H. S., Crohn, H., & Rodstein, E. (1981). Improving function of the remarried family system. *Journal of Marital and Family Therapy, 7,* 3-13.

Sanders, G. F., & Trygstad, D. W. (1989). Stepgrandparents and grandparents: The view from young adults. *Family Relations, 38,* 71-75.

Santrock, J. W., & Sitterle, K. (1987). Parent-child relationships in stepmother families. In K. Pasley & M. Ihinger-Tallman (Eds.), *Remarriage and stepparenting today: Current research and theory* (pp. 273-299). New York: Guilford.

Santrock, J. W., Warshak, R., Lindbergh, C., & Meadows, L. (1982). Children and parents' observed social behavior in stepfather families. *Child Development, 53,* 472-480.

Satir, V. (1972). *Peoplemaking.* Palo Alto, CA: Science & Behavior Books.

Scanzoni, J., Polonko, K., Teachman, J., & Thompson, L. (1989). *The sexual bond: Rethinking families and close relationships.* Newbury Park, CA: Sage.

Schultz, N. C., Schultz, C. L., & Olson, D. H. (1991). Couple strengths and stressors in simple and complex stepfamilies in Australia. *Journal of Marriage and the Family, 53,* 555-564.

Seltzer, J. A., & Bianchi, S. M. (1988). Children's contact with absent parents. *Journal of Marriage and the Family, 50,* 663-677.

Skolnick, A. (1991). *Embattled paradise.* New York: Basic Books.

Skyles, A. (1983). *Selected variables affecting stepparents' perceptions of dyadic adjustment in remarriage.* Unpublished doctoral dissertation, University of Wisconsin, Madison.

Smith, K. R., Zick, C. D., & Duncan, G. J. (1991). Remarriage patterns among recent widows and widowers. *Demography, 28,* 361-374.

Smith, R. M., Goslen, M. A., Byrd, A. J., & Reece, L. (1991). Self-other orientation and sex-role orientation of men and women who remarry. *Journal of Divorce and Remarriage, 15,* 3-31.

Smith, T. A. (1991). Family cohesion in remarried families. *Journal of Divorce and Remarriage, 17,* 49-66.

Smith, W. C. (1953). *The stepchild.* Chicago: University of Chicago Press.

Smock, P. J. (1990). Remarriage patterns of black and white women: Reassessing the role of educational attainment. *Demography, 27,* 467-473.

Spanier, G. B., & Furstenberg, F. F. (1987). Remarriage and reconstituted families. In M. B. Sussman & S. Steinmetz (Eds.), *Handbook of marriage and the family* (pp. 419-434). New York: Plenum.

Stacey, J. (1990). *Brave new families.* New York: Basic Books.

Straus, M., Gelles, R., & Steinmetz, S. (Eds.). (1980). *Behind closed doors: Violence in the American family.* New York: Anchor.

Sweet, J. (1991, November). *The demography of one-parent and stepfamilies changing marriage, remarriage, and reproductive patterns.* Paper presented at the Wingspread Conference on Remarried Families, Denver, CO.

Teachman, J. D. (1986). First and second marital dissolution: A decomposition exercise for whites and blacks. *Sociological Quarterly, 27,* 571-590.

Tenenbaum, J. D. (1991). Legislation for stepfamilies: The Family Law Section Standing Committee report. *Family Law Quarterly, 25*(10) 137.

Thompson, L. (1992). Feminist methodology for family studies. *Journal of Marriage and the Family, 54,* 3-18.

Thomson, E., McLanahan, S. S., & Curtin, R. B. (1992). Family structure, gender, and parental socialization. *Journal of Marriage and the Family, 54,* 368-378.

Tinsley, B., & Parke, R. (1987). Grandparents as interactive and social support agents for families with young infants. *International Journal of Aging and Human Development, 25,* 261-279.

Troll, L. (1983). Grandparents: The family watchdogs. In T. Brubaker (Ed.), *Family relationships in later life* (pp. 63-74). Beverly Hills, CA: Sage.

U.S. Bureau of the Census. (1992). *Marriage, divorce, and remarriage in the 1990s* (Current Population Reports, No. P23-180). Washington, DC: Government Printing Office.

Vemer, E., Coleman, M., Ganong, L., & Cooper, H. (1989). Marital satisfaction in remarriage: A meta-analysis. *Journal of Marriage and the Family, 51,* 713-725.

Vinick, B. H. (1978). Remarriage in old age. *Family Coordinator, 27,* 359-363.

Visher, E. B., & Visher, J. S. (1978). Common problems of stepparents and their spouses. *American Journal of Orthopsychiatry, 48,* 252-262.

Visher, E. B., & Visher, J. S. (1979). *Stepfamilies: A guide to working with stepparents and stepchildren.* New York: Brunner/Mazel.

Visher, E. B., & Visher, J. S. (1982). Children in stepfamilies. *Psychiatric Annals, 12,* 832-841.

Visher, E. B., & Visher, J. S. (1988). *Old loyalties, new ties: Therapeutic strategies with stepfamilies.* New York: Brunner/Mazel.

Visher, E. B., & Visher, J. S. (1990). Dynamics of successful stepfamilies. *Journal of Divorce and Remarriage, 14*(1), 3-12.

Visher, J. S., & Visher, E. B. (1991). Therapy with stepfamily couples. *Psychiatric Annals, 21,* 462-465.

Voydanoff, P. (1990). Economic distress and family relations: A review of the eighties. *Journal of Marriage and the Family, 52,* 1099-1115.

Wald, E. (1981). *The remarried family: Challenge and promise.* New York: Family Service Association of America.

Waldren, T., Bell, N. J., Peek, C. W., & Sorell, G. (1990). Cohesion and adaptability in postdivorce remarried and first-married families: Relationships with family stress and coping styles. *Journal of Divorce and Remarriage, 14*(1), 13-28.

Walker, K. N., & Messinger, L. (1979). Remarriage after divorce: Dissolution and reconstruction of family boundaries. *Family Process, 18,* 185-192.

Waller, W. (1930). *The old love and the new: Divorce and readjustment.* Philadelphia: Liveright.

Walsh, W. M. (1992). Twenty major issues in remarriage families. *Journal of Counseling and Development, 70,* 709-715.

Weddle, S. (1993). *The effect of nonresidential children's perceived physical and psychological presence on remarriage adjustment and affect.* Unpublished doctoral dissertation, University of Missouri.

Weitzman, L. (1988). Women and children last: The social and economic consequences of divorce law reforms. In S. Dornbusch & M. Strober (Eds.), *Feminism, children, and the new families* (pp. 212-248). New York: Guilford.

Weston, C. A., & Macklin, E. D. (1990). The relationship between former-spousal contact and remarital satisfaction in stepfather families. *Journal of Divorce and Remarriage, 14*(2), 25-47.

White, L. K., & Booth, A. (1985). The quality and stability of remarriages: The role of stepchildren. *American Sociological Review, 50,* 689-698.

White, L. K., & Reidmann, A. (1992). When the Brady Bunch grows up: Step-/half- and full sibling relationships in adulthood. *Journal of Marriage and the Family, 54,* 197-208.

Whiteside, M. F. (1982). Remarriage: A family developmental process. *Journal of Marital and Family Therapy, 4,* 59-68.

Whiteside, M. F. (1988). Creation of family identity through ritual performance in early remarriage. In E. Imber-Black, J. Roberts, & R. Whiting (Eds.), *Rituals in families and family therapy* (pp. 276-304). New York: Norton.

Whiteside, M. F. (1989). Family rituals as a key to kinship connections in remarried families. *Family Relations, 38*(1), 34-39.

Whitsett, D., & Land, H. (1992). Role strain, coping, and marital satisfaction of stepparents. *Families in Society: The Journal of Contemporary Human Services, 73,* 79-91.

Wilson, B. F., & Clarke, S. C. (1992). Remarriages: A demographic profile. *Journal of Family Issues, 13,* 123-141.

Wilson, M., & Daly, M. (1987). Risk of maltreatment of children living with stepparents. In R. J. Gelles & J. B. Lancaster (Eds.), *Child abuse and neglect: Biosocial dimensions* (pp. 215-232). Hawthorne, NY: Aldine.

Wineberg, H. (1990). Childbearing after remarriage. *Journal of Marriage and the Family, 52,* 31-38.

Wineberg, H. (1992). Childbearing and dissolution of the second marriage. *Journal of Marriage and the Family, 54,* 879-887.

Zick, C. D., & Smith, K. R. (1988). Recent widowhood, remarriage, and changes in economic well-being. *Journal of Marriage and the Family, 50,* 233-244.

Zill, N. (1988). Behavior, achievement, and health problems among children in stepfamilies: Findings from a national survey of child health. In E. M. Hetherington & J. D. Arasteh (Eds.), *Impact of divorce, single parenting, and stepparenting on children* (pp. 325-368). Hillsdale, NJ: Lawrence Erlbaum.

Zukow, P. G. (Ed.). (1989). *Sibling interaction across cultures: Theoretical and methodological issues.* New York: Springer Verlag.

Name Index

Subject Index

About the Authors

Marilyn Coleman, Ed.D., is Professor and former Chair of Human Development and Family Studies at the University of Missouri, Columbia. She received a B.S. in dietetics from Kansas State University, Manhattan; an M.S. in child development from the University of Missouri; and an Ed.D. in special education from the University of Missouri. She has been a member of the University of Missouri faculty since 1969. In addition to her administrative duties as department chair, she has taught courses on marriage and divorce, research methods, human development, and remarriage and stepparenting. She is editor of *Journal of Marriage and the Family* and also serves or has served on the editorial boards of *Family Relations, Journal of Family Issues, Lifestyles: Family and Economic Issues,* and *Home Economics Research Journal.* She has authored or coauthored many publications, including books, study guides, book chapters, and journal articles. She has won awards for research and leadership from the American Home Economics Association, and the University of Missouri has honored her with several research and teaching awards. Her research interests are remarriage and stepparenting, love, sex roles, and family structure stereotypes. She recently has begun a research program on family obligation (with Larry Ganong), and they also are conducting an evaluation of an early childhood intervention program for the Ewing Marion Kauffman Foundation.

Lawrence H. Ganong, Ph.D., is Professor of Nursing and Human Development and Family Studies at the University of Missouri, Columbia. He received a B.A. in psychology from Washburn University, Topeka, Kansas; an M.S. in family studies from Kansas State University, Manhattan; an M.Ed. in counseling psychology from the University of Missouri, Columbia; and a Ph.D. in family studies from the University of Missouri. He held a faculty position at Central Missouri State University, Warrensburg, prior to joining the University of Missouri faculty in 1980. He teaches courses in family dynamics and intervention, theories of human development, and research methods. He also regularly teaches a graduate course on remarriage and stepparenting with his wife and frequent coauthor, Marilyn Coleman. He serves or has served on the editorial boards of several professional journals, such as *Journal of Marriage and the Family, Family Relations, Journal of Family Issues,* and *Journal of Family and Economic Issues.* He has authored and coauthored two books, a study guide, and approximately 100 articles in professional and popular publications. His two primary research interests are remarriage and stepparenting, and family-related stereotypes, although he also has conducted research on sex roles, love, and parent education. Although he no longer practices, he is trained as both a counselor and as a family mediator.